"*Soomaaliya* is a beautiful, lyrical book, not just an exploration but an evocation of Somali food. Ifrah has that rare combination of tenderness and authority; she's a wonderful storyteller. This book—and the cuisine it captures—deserves to be celebrated far and wide."

—RUBY TANDOH, food writer and author of *All Consuming*

"As anticipated by anyone who's read her work, Ifrah F. Ahmed's debut cookbook is not just a collection of recipes, but a historical and cultural narrative that beautifully situates Somali cuisine in its contexts—both at home and in diaspora. *Soomaaliya* is a foundational work of food writing."

—ALICIA KENNEDY, author of *No Meat Required*

"Ifrah F. Ahmed's excellent first cookbook *Soomaaliya* highlights the importance of all cuisines to be represented with respect to the beauty and realities of their cultural roots, while acknowledging the powerful acts of the diasporic communities in both preserving traditional food and adapting to their new places of living. Through delicious recipes and thoughtful portraits of Somali individuals and small businesses, Ifrah has crafted a one-of-a-kind cookbook. When I saw the recipe of my favourite Somali dish, bariis isku karis, my appetite smiled!"

—FADI KATTAN, chef and author of *Bethlehem*

"Ifrah F. Ahmed's debut cookbook is a knockout—she pays rich, expansive tribute to one of the world's greatest and most under-documented cuisines. She has, in doing so, set a high standard for any future books on the subject of Somali cooking."

—MAYUKH SEN, author of *Love, Queenie* and *Taste Makers*

SOOMAALIYA
𐒈𐒝𐒑𐒛𐒐𐒘𐒕𐒖

SOOMAALIYA

𐒈𐒝𐒑𐒛𐒐𐒘𐒕𐒖

Food, Memory, and Migration: A Cookbook

Ifrah F. Ahmed

Hardie Grant
NORTH AMERICA

Aqoon la'aan waa iftiin la'aan.
The absence of knowledge is the absence of light.
—SOMALI PROVERB

Food is everything we are. It's an extension of nationalist feeling, ethnic feeling, your personal history, your province, your region, your tribe, your grandma. It's inseparable from those from the get-go.

—ANTHONY BOURDAIN

CONTENTS

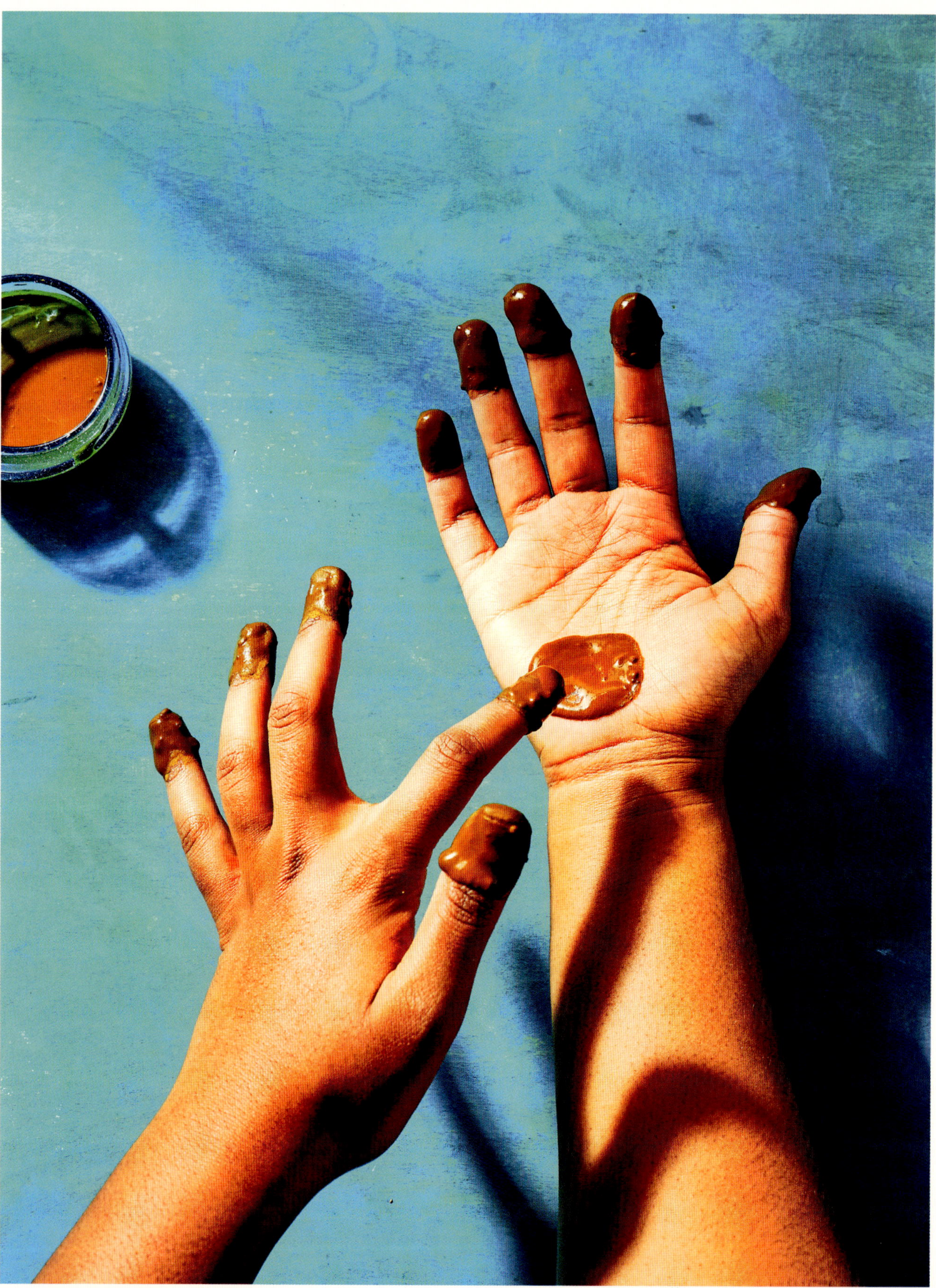

Soo Dhawoow

A WELCOME AND AN INTRODUCTION

Our words are our record keepers. In them, our histories, our languages, and our truths are contained.

In Somali culture, knowledge is passed down orally—through songs, stories, recipes, and more. Our oral tradition is such a fundamental part of our culture that even the names of each generation are passed down this way. Historically, Somalis who met anywhere in the world could figure out if they shared lineage because they would each have memorized the names of their patrilineal ancestors going back hundreds of years. This oral tradition, called *abtirsi*, is the thread that has long held together the fabric of who we are as Somalis.

But what happens when this intergenerational cultural transmission is interrupted? For many Somalis, the transfer of language and culture (including recipes and foods) was disrupted—and in some cases severed—by the Somali Civil War that began in 1991 and the resulting mass migration out of Somalia over the course of the next thirty years. We became a people scattered, a global diaspora of millions.

I was born in Mogadishu, Somalia, and came to the United States as a refugee in 1996. My story and that of my family closely mirror the experience of the more than two million other Somali people in the diaspora. We were families who were living peacefully in our homeland one day, and fleeing to any country that would have us the next. We were individuals who resettled elsewhere and tried to reimagine our lives while also attempting to hang on to the pieces of our identity amid the chaos. Somali refugees created our own safe spaces in our new homelands by establishing community hubs like halal grocery stores, cafés, malls, restaurants, and mosques. In these places, we could connect with one another and our culture could live on among us.

Despite the creation of these community hubs, many members of the international Somali population cannot speak the language, do not know our histories, and cannot make our traditional foods. And because of Somalis' historic reliance on a rich oral tradition, few Somali cookbooks—or even other written documents of Somali cookery—exist. Resettlement in the diaspora has made it so that many Somalis no longer have either the opportunity to learn from elders or family with whom to continue these practices.

When those few resources that document Somali cuisine *do* exist—such as the 2010s-era pioneering Somali food blog *Xawaash*—they have found a hungry global audience. But on the whole, Somali cuisine remains largely unknown to many non-Somali people.

THE HORN OF AFRICA

Approximate Area Inhabited by Somali People

It has not yet enjoyed comparable representation in traditional food media or in the restaurant landscape as the cuisines of neighboring countries like Ethiopia. When Somali food is presented, it is often flattened into the general category of "East African" cuisine, our unique dishes misattributed to other, neighboring countries.

With this book, as with much of my work, I hope to extend the reality of Somali food into the world. That reality is storied, rich, compelling, and unique.

Somalia's geographical location in the Horn of Africa positioned it to become a hub of international trade for centuries, trading with ancient Egypt, Persia, India, Rome, and pre–Ming Dynasty China. The people, products, and foods of a whole hemisphere passed through our ports. More locally, commonalities with Yemeni, Ethiopian, and Swahili foods can also be found in Somali cuisine. And more recently, Somali agriculture and cuisine were shaped by the nineteenth-century colonizing presence of France, England, and Italy. The Italian colonial government, in particular, introduced mass production of cash crops like sugarcane and bananas, used forced labor, and incorporated agricultural technology in ways that forever changed how Somalis grew and consumed food.

I learned Somali cooking from my mother. Upon our resettlement in the rainy city of Seattle, my mother, despite being the breadwinner and working two jobs, began a campaign to immerse us in our culture. For me, that meant weekly cooking lessons and instruction in Somali culture. I loved watching my hooyo—my mother—in the kitchen, conjuring up smells and tastes that were intimate and familiar.

I have early memories of pounding green cardamom pods and thick chunks of gingerroot with a mortar and pestle as I learned how to make a perfect cup of shaah (spiced tea). These lessons continued until I went to college. In between maintaining a perfect 4.0, working at my public library, and attending both dugsi (weekend Islamic school) and clandestine DIY punk rock shows, I learned how to expertly swirl ladles of batter into spongy pieces of canjeero (sour fermented pancake) to be paired with shaah for a classic Somali breakfast and how to fry sambuus (dumplings) to a golden crunch. I didn't always love these lessons. They sometimes felt like a burden I bore because of my gender, but I now realize they were my mother's way of making sure I never forgot that I'll always be *Somali*.

My mother's cooking lessons became my stepping stones into the larger culinary world. During my teen years, I became immersed in food culture, devouring Food Network shows, chef biographies, and all things Anthony Bourdain. Still, I didn't see food as a legitimate career path. Having internalized immigrant/refugee family expectations of seeking out a career in law, medicine, or engineering, I graduated from college with a political science degree and a pre-law minor. From there, I worked for Seattle Public Schools, mentoring and assisting newly arrived Somali refugee students while studying for the LSAT and then applying to law school.

Later I got married and moved to Brooklyn, New York, for law school, with the intention of becoming a human rights lawyer. I threw myself into the rigors of the law, learning about it in the classroom and via my volunteer work and legal internships at organizations such as the Center for Constitutional Rights. During it all, cooking was

CARLYLE CRUISE
2007

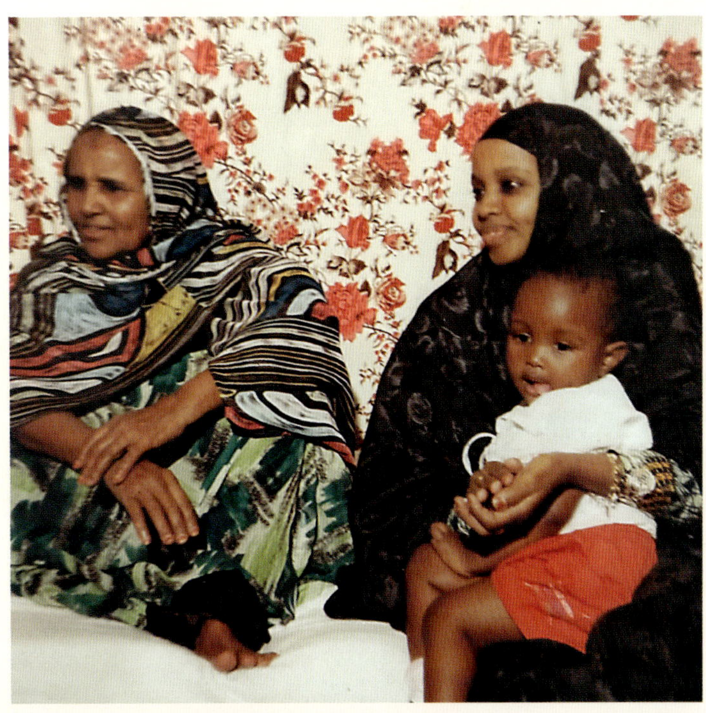

a creative and emotional outlet that helped me process the brutal reality, including violence, that I witnessed in the lives of my clients.

I brought homemade sambuus, basbaas, and other traditional Somali foods to my classmates, to my legal internships on Somali Independence Day, and even to my neighborhood block parties and community garden in Bed-Stuy, where I had become a gardener and a member. This allowed my creative side to flourish and was an opportunity for me to share my passion for Somali cuisine. During this time, I also co-founded a pioneering feminist arts and culture magazine called *Araweelo Abroad*, which celebrated the creative achievements of Somali women and focused on preserving our cultural contributions.

After two years, I realized that law school wasn't for me. The work I was involved in had also become too emotionally taxing, and the experiences of my clients weighed heavily on me. But cooking for others felt like an act of service. It reminded me of why I had wanted to become a lawyer but didn't compel me to constantly carry the trauma and heartache of my community.

In 2018, I went on a homecoming trip to Somalia with my mother—my first time back since leaving as a child. The trip was life-changing. After so long, I was again surrounded by people speaking my language—people who looked like me—and, most importantly, by my culture. I soaked up all I could, immersing myself in the history and stories behind the culinary traditions I grew up with. I began to imagine a future in which I could blend my love of food with the training I had received from my mother and my commitment to preserving Somali culture.

Back in Brooklyn, I dedicated myself to a full-time career in food. In 2019, I launched my traveling culinary pop-up, MILK & MYRRH, where I served reimagined Somali cuisine to sold-out crowds in cities like Los Angeles, New York, and Seattle. I cooked canjeero burritos, fish suqaar, and salmon sambuus, classic Somali foods informed by diasporic migration and reimagined with the available seasonal produce. As I held more and more pop-ups, I had the opportunity to speak with many people, both Somalis and non-Somalis, who felt connected to the mission behind my work and who loved my unique approach to making, sharing, and preserving Somali cuisine.

In 2020, I not only became a mother but also began writing down my recipes. With the birth of my daughter, I felt a renewed sense of urgency to carry on my own mother's mission of teaching Somali culture, not only for my child but for all future generations of Somalis.

As I navigated new motherhood and a pandemic that had shut down the whole world, I began publishing recipes in the *Washington Post* and the *New York Times*, where I am a regular contributor to the food section and share my expertise in Somali cuisine. I also wrote for publications like *Vogue*, *LA Times*, *Eater*, and *TASTE*, where my essays on food, memory, and the Somali diaspora further connected me with people excited to see our cuisine and culture written about and shared widely.

Without fully realizing it, I had also been writing a book. *Soomaaliya* is a cookbook of Somali recipes—largely in their most traditional iterations and some reflecting how dishes have evolved as Somalis have formed a global diaspora. But it's also a book that considers how colonialism, migration, and war have impacted our culture and our food.

In addition to classic and modern recipes, this book spotlights Somalis who work to preserve the Somali culinary arts—people like Leila Adde and Abdullahi Kassim, founders of the pioneering Somali food blog *Xawaash*; Jamal Hashi, a Minnesota-based Somali chef and a subject of Apple TV's *Little America*; Barlin Ali, author of *Somali Cuisine*; restaurateur Liban Tahlil, owner of the popular London-based restaurant Sabiib; Muhsen Hirabe, owner of the largest banana farm in Somalia; and Abdisalan Warsame, a former camel herder and current professor at Somali National University.

Soomaaliya is a book that draws from and pays homage to the oral tradition of my culture, and one that I hope will serve as a resource that will endure and inspire future generations of Somalis. I am writing it so that Somali culinary traditions are not lost to the next generation. While this book is not a repository of all Somali dishes (no one book could be!), it is my wish that it serve as a valued source of Somali recipes and culinary practices for all Somalis, both at home and in the diaspora. I hope it will also be a valuable resource for anyone who wants to learn more about Somali food and how to make it.

In the end, I want you to walk away with an understanding of Somalia's rich and ancient cuisine, including how it's been shaped by colonialism, war, and diasporic migration and how Somalis have fought to keep our culinary traditions alive. Most importantly, I hope you are inspired by this book to be a living part of those traditions as a cook, a host, and a lover of food and culture.

CHAPTER 1

SOMALIA AND ITS CUISINE

Somalia, once called a "Nation of Bards" by explorer Richard Burton, has been known by many names over the centuries: Regio Cinnamafore (Land of Cinnamon) by the ancient Romans, Punt by the ancient Egyptians, Barbaria by the ancient Greeks, and Berberi by the ancient Arabs. Her people, the Soomaalis, know her as Soomaaliya, a name with several possible etymologies. One theory is that the name derives from Irir Samaale, the name of the common forefather of several major clans. Another holds that the word *Samaale*, like *Sab* (the name of another Somali ancestor), is actually a description of the different ways the people now known as Somalis lived, with *Samaale* meaning "a man who owns and travels with livestock" and *Sab* meaning "where the people live in one place and do not travel or own animals."

Other theories connect the name either to the Somali phrase *soo maal*, which means "go and milk," or to the Arabic *zawamal*, or "wealthy," describing how ancient Arabs viewed Somalis, with their abundant livestock. According to historian Mohamed Nuuh Ali, the word *Somali* appears first in the eleventh-century writings of Muslim cartographer al-Idrisi. The next recorded references to Somalis came from King Yeshaq of Abyssinia (modern Ethiopia), who ruled from 1414 to 1429 and used the word in a song celebrating his victory in battle.

Somalia is one of the most homogeneous countries on the African continent. Its inhabitants mostly speak af Soomaali, the nation's official language since 1972, and 99.9 percent share one religion, Islam (mostly Sunni Islam), with a tiny minority of Christians. A dozen or so distinct Bantu languages such as Mushunguli and Chimwiini are also spoken, along with some Italian and English (relics of colonial rule) and Arabic (the country's second official language).

There are about eighteen million people currently living in Somalia and about two million living abroad in the Somali diaspora. Of these twenty million people, 15 to 20 percent are ethnic minorities such as Somali Bantus, Reer Xamar, Bajuni, and Arab Somalis or occupational castes like the Gabooye, Tumaal, and Yibir.

Somalis are divided into many different patrilineal clans, the five largest being the Isaaq, Hawiye, Darood, Dir, and Rahanweyn. The clan system is the backbone of Somali society and culture; the clans provide a social identity and membership within society, allowing individuals to navigate politics, resolve conflicts, and manage personal and family matters such as marriages and funerals.

Somalia's geographic location in the Horn of Africa has historically made it a key player in geopolitics, and its coastline (the longest in mainland Africa, with many ports) has been an important stop on global trade routes since as early as the third millennium BCE. Mogadishu is an ancient port city, founded sometime between the sixth and tenth centuries CE. Somalia's interior is hilly in the north and flatter in the central and southern regions. As an equatorial country, it doesn't have much seasonal temperature variation; gu (spring) and dayr (autumn) are the rainy seasons, while xagaa (summer) and jilaal (winter) are typically dry.

Milk and meat are at the heart of the Somali diet, and pastoralism is highly esteemed in Somali society. Somali consumption of milk and meat was first recorded as early as the fifth century BCE by the ancient Greeks. A ninth-century CE Chinese travel document noted that the people of Berbera (the Horn of Africa) consumed no cereals but did eat meat. A thirteenth-century account by Chao Ju-kua remarked on the many camels and sheep Somalis owned and their consumption of milk and camel meat.

While pastoralism has been both a way of life and a status indicator in Somalia for thousands of years, farming has always existed alongside it, particularly in southern Somalia. Farmers have been viewed as a lower class by pastoralists, who associated land cultivation with slavery. Farming is centered along rivers, and crops include beans, sesame, corn, cereals like millet and varieties of sorghum, and papaya. Along the coastal areas, fruits and vegetables are grown and the diet incorporates seafood, including tuna, shark, and turtle—foods absent from the pastoralists' diet.

Weather and landscape have long shaped the Somali nomadic way of life, with the seasons dictating where nomads could go, and how. The ancient nomadic tradition has been badly disrupted by the ongoing Somali Civil War and is in decline. A 2014 United Nations survey estimated that 26 percent of Somalis at that time were pastoral nomads, 42 percent were urban dwellers, 23 percent lived in rural areas, and 9 percent were internally displaced.

ANCIENT SOMALIA: AGRICULTURE AND TRADE

Somalia's early history saw the establishment of thriving coastal cities that became hubs of international trade. Somalis had trading relationships with other ancient civilizations such as the Greeks, Babylonians, and Egyptians; trading goods included spices and the prized gum resins frankincense and myrrh that were produced in the region.

The Laas Geel cave paintings in northern Somalia dating back five thousand years depict pastoral scenes that include livestock such as camels. Other important archaeological finds include the remnants of a burial ground in the Paleolithic city of Jaleelo, located in modern-day Somaliland.

Various theories have arisen about the origins of the Somali people. Historian Raphael C. Njoku writes: "Somalia is a nation with a history that stretches back more than ten millennia to the beginnings of human civilization." Somalis migrated from neither the Ethiopian highlands nor the Arab Peninsula (as previously thought), but are indigenous to the region and migrated south in the first century CE.

Evidence shows the beginnings of Somali trade with the outside world in the third century BCE, with ancient Egyptian expeditions to the Land of Punt (Somalia). According to Abdurahman Abdullahi Baadiyow's *Making Sense of Somali History*, a hierographic diary shows ships sent by Queen Hatshepsut to the Land of Punt in 1478 BCE. There were not only trade links between Punt and Egypt, but also deep cultural and religious ties. The Egyptians believed that Punt was their place of origin, and many ancient Egyptian and modern-day Somali words share roots.

Baadiyow states that in the fifth century BCE, the Greek historian Herodotus described "Macrobians" in the south of Egypt—"tall and handsome" warriors, who lived long lives of up to 120 years due to their "diet of meat and milk." In addition to this diet of meat and milk, ancient Somalis, who knew how to cultivate ancient grains and turn them into bread, porridge, and flour, were also consuming sorghum, wheat, coffee, chickpeas, and barley. According to Baadiyow, camels were likely domesticated in the Horn between the second and third millennium BCE. Agronomist Nikolai Vavilov has found that the Horn is also home to thirty-eight indigenous crop plants, including spices.

THE MEDIEVAL PERIOD: ISLAM AND INTERCONTINENTAL TRADE

Somalia's medieval period was a time of great change that cemented these lands as an important part of the global economy. Islam's introduction to the region and the establishment of sultanates after 1000 CE connected Somalis to the Muslim and Arab worlds. These connections allowed people and products to move across the Indian Ocean—routes along which Somalia commanded several important ports, including Mogadishu, Baraawe, Zeila, and Berbera, the last two having long been documented as thriving commercial ports in *Periplus of the Erythraean Sea*, a sailing logbook authored by an anonymous Greek sailor in the first century CE. The trade and migration that accompanied the spread of Islam would profoundly shape Somali cuisine, economy, culture, and identity thereafter.

Somalis converted to Islam around the seventh century CE, leaving behind an indigenous monotheism that worshipped a god called Waaq. It is debated whether Somalis converted following the arrival of the Prophet Muhammad's companions in the Horn or whether the religion was brought by multiple waves of settlements of Arab merchants to the Somali coast later on. Among its first footholds was the coastal city of Zeila, where the ruins of Masjid al-Qiblatayn, one of the oldest mosques in Africa, still stand today. By the thirteenth century, most Somalis were Muslims, but even with their embrace of Islam, Somali identity was not lost—instead it was the immigrants who became "Somalized."

In the fourteenth century CE, Ibn Battuta, a Moroccan traveling throughout the Muslim world, visited Mogadishu. He documented the Somali diet as one centered around grains, fish, meat, vegetables, and poultry, which was "consumed in large quantities" and gave an "impression of great wealth." This wealth was evidenced by the inhabitants of Mogadishu "slaughter[ing] hundreds of camels every day." Battuta also wrote about being welcomed with a large dish of rice topped with "fowl fat, meat, fish, and legumes."

While Arabs and Persians had an ongoing trade presence on the Somali coast during this period, Portuguese explorers like Vasco da Gama also recognized the value of Somalia's location. The Portuguese engaged Somalis in years long battles beginning in 1499, attempting to take important port cities like Baraawe and Zeila. In the sixteenth century, Ahmad ibn Ibrahim al-Ghazi (known in Somali as Gurey), an imam of the Adal Sultanate, led a military campaign—a holy war—against the encroachment of the Abyssinians and the Portuguese.

Somalia's trading relationships in the medieval and early modern eras were not limited to the Muslim world, however, since its valuable ports made it a part of the larger ocean economy. Southeast Asia and ancient China in particular had long-standing trade

relationships out of the Banaadir port. In fact, Chinese documentation of Somalis goes as far back as the ninth century, and later, Somali explorer Sa'id of Mogadishu even traveled to China during the Yuan dynasty.

Ibn Battuta's consumption of rice in fourteenth-century Mogadishu also shows that Somalia already had a trade connection with Asia. The trade relationship went both ways; and the movement of products and goods was of mutual benefit for Somalia and Asia, with a flow of frankincense, myrrh, coffee, livestock, spices, gold, and ivory from East Africa, and of rice, swords, and textiles (and, later, firearms) from India and China.

Somalia's acceptance of Islam undoubtedly strengthened its relations with the rest of the Muslim world, cementing its importance in global trade. And it also shaped Somalia's food and culture—and its economy—forever.

THE COLONIAL PERIOD: CONQUEST, RULE, AND RESISTANCE

Somalia's modern age was shaped by the race among various European powers to colonize Somali territories—including the fertile south, the heart of Somalia's agricultural production and home to the important port cities Mogadishu and Baraawe. Within a span of decades starting in the mid-nineteenth century, foreign powers had occupied much of the African continent, including Somalia.

In 1839, the British occupied Aden, a city in Yemen; fifteen years later, British explorer Richard Burton traveled to Zeila in northern Somalia. In 1869, the Suez Canal opened, and by 1875, Egypt had begun occupying northern coastal towns in Somalia like Berbera and Kismayo (it later withdrew), while Zanzibar intermittently ruled the southern coast. Colonizers' interest in the region continued to grow, and in 1884, European powers held the infamous Berlin Conference, and the scramble for Africa was on.

Through forced expansion, the colonial powers began partitioning the continent. In 1884, the British signed treaties with the Isaaq, establishing the British Somaliland Protectorate; this ensured them a supply of meat to their colony in Aden and safe passage in the region. Later, the British would take the southwestern region of the Somali territories and incorporate it into British Kenya as the Northern Frontier District.

Between 1862 and 1864, France signed treaties with the Ethiopian Afar clan and the Somali Issa clan, eventually establishing French Somaliland in 1896. In the south in 1889, Italy also exploited regional tensions to sign both an agreement with the Sultanate of Hobyo and a treaty with the rival Majeerteen Sultanate. The Italian stake in Somalia continued to grow until 1941, as they took more and more land, notably the abundant Banaadir coast in the south. Baraawe, on the Banaadir coast, had for centuries been a powerful trading and transit center for goods and people traveling via the Indian Ocean. This made it important for imperialists like the Italians, the British, and the Sultanate of Zanzibar, who were all looking to expand their empires.

A recently consolidated Ethiopian state joined the French, Italians, and British in dividing up territory in the Horn of Africa. In the 1897 Anglo-Abyssinian Treaty, the British granted Ethiopia the ancestral Somali lands of Hawd and the Ogaden. This was without Somali consent and in violation of the agreements European powers had made with Somali clans and sultanates. (The Ogaden was added back to Italian Somaliland in 1936 after the Italians invaded Ethiopia, then returned to Ethiopia by the British in 1948, despite the protest of ethnic Somalis in the region.) With this, the imperial partition of Somali lands was complete.

COLONIAL RULE AND ECONOMY

The colonial period in Somalia was a time of wholesale transformation. Notably, Italian colonial rulers established a plantation system, which fundamentally changed Somali agriculture, labor, and foodways. (It also sowed seeds of the independence movement.)

Somalis fiercely fought colonial rule, and among their most powerful weapons was their rejection of the colonizers' notions of European racial superiority. Somalis viewed themselves as their colonizers' racial equals or superiors. This frustrated the British in particular: It meant that their usual tactics of dividing Indigenous populations against one another failed.

In 1899, religious leader Sayyid Mohammed Abdullah Hassan (dubbed the "Mad Mullah" by the British) began a resistance movement called the Dervish Movement. Hassan used shared Somali ethnic identity and Islamic religious values to rally support for his movement across clan lines and against the non-Somali colonial invaders. The first Dervish victory happened at Jigjiga, the Somali capital city of the Ethiopian-occupied Ogaden region. This guerrilla uprising against colonial forces lasted until 1920, when the British launched a land and air offensive, bombing Hassan and his troops. When he died of influenza in 1920, his passing marked the end of the Dervish Movement.

The British presence in northern Somalia and the decades-long war had a lasting impact on the economy and environment and led to the displacement of much of the population. According to scholar Ahmed Ibrahim Awale, over two hundred thousand people perished in these wars. The effect on the environment exacerbated cyclical drought conditions and led to years of further conflict. (The period between 1909 and 1912 is called the Xaaraama-cune, "time of filth eating.")

While the Dervish movement was limited to the north, it planted the seeds of the pan-Somali movement that would eventually bloom into Somali nationalism. From 1890 to 1926, a guerrilla movement called the Banaadir resistance (also known as the Biimaal revolt) took place in Italian Somaliland in response to continued colonial expansion. Religious leaders Sheikh Abdi Abikar Gafle and Ma'alin Mursal Abdi Yusuf spearheaded a movement to keep the Italians out of the Marka region in the south. Despite efforts to quash it, this resistance persevered and received assistance from the Dervish movement.

Meanwhile, the Italians doubled down on their economic development in Somalia. The Italian state first entrusted the colony to Filonardi & Company, run by the former Italian consul to Zanzibar. By 1898, the Società Anonima Commerciale Italiana del Benadir replaced the Filonardi Company as the entity in charge of Italian Somaliland. Italy bought the Banaadir ports in 1905, and the Italian Parliament united all the areas they controlled in southern Somalia in 1908.

Beginning in 1919, the Italians established hundreds of plantations on land they had seized by the Juba and Shabelle Rivers. Prior to this plantation era, independent farmers in the Juba Valley area grew grain crops and traded the extra food they produced with people in the coastal towns.

Agricultural work was done by enslaved people, tenant farmers, or free farmers. In the Shabelle River area, Somali Bantu communities grew corn, sesame, and beans; constructed beehives to harvest honey; and kept cattle herds for meat, milk, and butter.

Slavery was a crucial part of the Banaadir region's economy in this era. More than fifty thousand enslaved people were brought to southern Somalia between 1800 and 1890. Two concurrent slave trades, in East Africa and along the Swahili coast, brought enslaved people from Ethiopia, Central Africa, and southern East Africa to Banaadir. The clans in the Shabelle area used this slave labor to maximize agricultural output, and later, European colonizers used the pre-existing slave labor system to enrich the colonial economy.

In 1904, Italy abolished slavery in its colonies; this angered pastoral Somalis, who claimed they had a religious entitlement to slave ownership, or hanti property. Historian Lee V. Cassanelli writes that the Italians assumed that the abolishment of slavery would mean that native Somalis would be the workforce on the European-owned farms. Instead, according to historian Diana Garvin, Somalis refused to do paid farm work as "a matter of anti-colonial principle." An agricultural survey from that time found that "the Somali is too proud . . . and too Muslim to work—they had always made the slaves do the agricultural work."

Occupations such as blacksmithing, hunting, shoemaking, and weaving had caste (or class) associations—they were not for the noble classes. Speaking of the societal dichotomy between "noble" and "outcast" lineages, Iman Mohamed writes that "the exclusion of occupational groups from *Soomaalinimo* [Somali identity] was embedded in the customary laws of Somali communities." Not surprisingly, the Somali refusal to submit to Italian political authority (due to the fact that they didn't need wages/income and were used to subsistence labor and usually bartered for goods) led the Italians to complain that the Somalis acted "as if they were on par with Europeans and held all the power."

Since abolition had precipitated a labor shortage that the colonial administration had not expected and could not otherwise solve, they not only turned a blind eye to the continuation of slavery in the region but used forced labor themselves. They designated certain Somalis—largely Somali Bantus—as *liberti*; these were members of "groups living in the riverine areas [with] perceived racial difference from pastoralist Somalis," in Iman Mohamed's words. The liberti were subject to forced labor on Italian-controlled farms, and, eventually, the Italians began to "recruit" from other populations as well.

The colonial administration, taking advantage of Somalia's ideal climate, had undertaken the large-scale production and export of bananas, sugar, and cotton, among other crops. The administration wanted Somalis to grow crops for local consumption because they didn't want to pay for imports, but they disrupted local production due to how much labor was diverted to Italian plantations. The long-standing export trade of Somali grain crops to the Arabian Peninsula (which had once earned it the nickname of "the grain coast") collapsed.

It became more and more difficult for Somalis to produce crops on their own land. To avoid labor conscription, farmers would abandon their own farms for villages along the Juba River, or they would go to religious Islamic settlements called jammaacooyin. Some Somalis returned to their former masters to work as servants. The decimation of Somali farm production paired with the colonialists' prioritization of cash crops led to increased food insecurity for many.

In 1911, Italy passed laws that gave Italian farmers Somali land to farm (for a fee). In 1920, Prince Luigi Amedeo established a company, the Società Agricola Italo-Somala (SAIS), to manage the Villaggio Duca degli Abruzzi, a new agricultural settlement named after him that initially grew cotton, then sugarcane, and later bananas. SAIS was a success and set the standard for colonial banana plantations for the next twenty years.

Throughout the 1920s, the Italian fascist government distributed land in Janaale to Italians as part of an effort to make agriculture the heart of the colonial economy. Initially, workers in these plantations were paid (albeit irregularly), and were permitted to leave after a month-long shift. Soon, however, a new system called *compartecipazione* (also known as the colonya), turned paid workers into sharecroppers who had a small piece of land on which to live and to grow crops. Entire families were now involved, and single people had an economic incentive to marry and reproduce. To meet worker housing needs, "company villages" were also built.

Adults and children worked a minimum eight-hour workday, under the constant surveillance of Italian managers and Somali foremen. They could not leave without prior permission or select their own work schedules. While the Italians felt the colonya system was humane and of mutual benefit, Somalis felt that this new system was exploitative and that it was a step down from their old way of life. Those who sought to escape faced violent beatings or arrest when caught. The threat of punishment and the constant surveillance created an environment of fear amongst the workers.

In 1927, Italian Somaliland began exporting bananas to Italy—introducing the fruit to many Italians for the first time. And after the collapse of the cotton industry in 1929, bananas became the crown jewel cash crop in the colonial economy—all due to land theft and forced labor. By 1933, Janaale (the heart of banana production in Somalia) produced ten times more bananas than any other Somali plantations, and in 1935, the Royal Banana Monopoly was established in Mogadishu to export Somali bananas. By 1938, bananas were available in every part of Italy. The colonial experimentation around banana farming for export (along with the import of Italian foods like pasta beginning in the early 1900s) would change Somali agricultural economy—and cuisine—forever. Garvin writes that, to this day in Italy, "bananas continue to be potent and contested symbols, often as racist shorthand for Africanness."

THE ROAD TO INDEPENDENCE

Following the first wave of Somali anti-colonial resistance at the turn of the 20th century, colonial regimes aimed to consolidate control over their Somali colonies, with limited success until the 1920s. The decades from the 1920s to the 1960s would be marked by attempts to bring order to the colonies via worker oppression and forced agricultural development. The period was further shaped by the continued struggle for independence, which laid the groundwork for the birth of a new nation.

In 1923, Cesare Maria De Vecchi became the first Fascist governor of Italian Somaliland. He sought to bring "Fascist order" to the colony, changing the administrative staff of the colony, introducing the lire as the official currency, forcibly disarming the clans, and establishing a Zaptié police force to control agricultural laborers on colonial plantations.

De Vecchi wanted to leave a legacy. He set up businesses in Janaale and built large infrastructure projects: roads, a railway, and a dam. The colony went from having fewer than five agricultural concessions, or settler-controlled plantations, in 1920 to having 115 in 1933. Most of those concessions focused on banana production.

Despite the Italian government's denial that it was using forced labor, this level of agricultural output would have been impossible without the colonizers' coercion of Somali workers and alienation of native lands. For example, in this period, it was illegal for Somalis to refuse police orders. So, when Zaptié police forcibly (and routinely) escorted workers to areas where there was a labor shortage, there was no recourse for those workers.

In the early years of his governorship, De Vecchi made substantial—and aggressive—expansionist moves. In 1924, the British ceded Jubaland to the Italians. In 1925, the once-powerful Hobyo Sultanate surrendered to De Vecchi's governance. In 1926, the

governor urged a brutal response to the El Hagi Revolt, and two hundred Somalis were slaughtered. In 1927, after fighting a bitter war against the Italian colonial state, the head of the Majeerteen Sultanate gave up his rule, and northeastern Somalia was joined to the Italian colony. Italy also began expanding into the occupied Ogaden territory, inciting the Somali population and increasing tensions with the Ethiopians.

In 1934 and 1935, Italy prepared their Somali colony for war with Ethiopia. Mussolini's new governor, Rodolfo Graziani, recruited thousands of Somalis, including pastoralists, despite theoretically needing them to maintain a level of pastoralism for the economy. By 1935, an estimated fifty thousand Italians lived in Somalia. This year also brought the founding of Jam'iyat 'Atiyyat al-Rahman (Gift of God Society), a club in British Somaliland that would be the precursor for the anti-colonial Somali National League (SNL).

In May of 1936, Italy conquered Addis Ababa, and Ethiopia (including the occupied Somali territory of Ogaden) became part of the Empire of Italian East Africa alongside Eritrea and Italian Somaliland. When Italy and England entered World War II on opposite sides, fighting over their respective East African territories ensued, with the British bombing Italian Somaliland, and the Italians invading British Kenya and capturing British Somaliland. With a larger portion of the Somali territories under the Italian flag, Iman Mohamed writes that the Italians went on to promote the idea of "Greater Somalia." However, the British recaptured their territories in 1941 and held them, along with the Ogaden, until 1948, and Italian Somaliland until 1950.

A second wave of anti-colonial resistance began in the 1940s, and it brought about the 1946 formation of the Somali Youth Club (later called the Somali Youth League, or SYL), the first nationalist party. The SYL's anti-clan values, nationalist identity, anger over colonial rule, and desire for Somali reunification made it an influential political party across all the Somali territories. In Italian Somaliland, it had a membership of ninety-three thousand people at its height and established a women's branch in the 1950s.

One area of focus for the SYL was challenging the de facto segregation in bars and restaurants as well as forcing the integration of buses and cinemas that legally did not allow Somalis and Europeans to occupy the same space. Things came to a head in 1947, when the SYL attempted to desegregate buses, bars, and cinemas through a series of demonstrations by Somali youth in Mogadishu and Merca entering Italian bars and restaurants. Reactions were mixed, with negative responses from colonizers and some native Somalis alike: Italians who remained after the establishment of British rule asked for enforcement of the old policies and religious Somali elders feared the youth would be exposed to forbidden foods.

After the Second World War and the Italian defeat, the international community deliberated over the future of Italian Somaliland. Somali nationalists advocated for a Greater Somalia, a view that was briefly endorsed in an unsuccessful British proposal for the Somali territories to remain unified under a trusteeship in 1946. When the Four Powers Commission (comprising the World War II victors France, the USSR, the US, and Great Britain) arrived in Mogadishu in 1948 to inquire about the political wishes of the colony's inhabitants, SYL members circulated a leaflet that said, in part, "Do we want the return of colonisation under a foreign government? NO! After 50 years of colonisation what have we learned? WE HAVE LEARNT HOW TO EAT MACARONI!"

The SYL clashed with Italian supporters, leading to a number of deaths including that of Hawo Taako (Xaawo Taako Cismaan), a female SYL member who is held as a political martyr. In 1949, another demonstration called Dhagaxtuur, or the "stone throwing," took place. Statues depicting Xaawo Taako and the Dhagaxtuur would be erected in later years, cementing both as anti-colonial symbols. Ultimately, the commission sent the question to the UN and, in 1950, the Italians were granted trusteeship of Somali lands, with the goal of Somali independence in 1960.

On June 26, 1960, British Somaliland gained independence and became Somaliland. Italian Somaliland gained independence on July 1 and reunited with Somaliland to become the United Republic of Somalia with Aden Abdulle Osman as the first president. Though Somalis advocated for a state that included all the colonial territories where the Somali people lived, Somali territories in Ethiopia, Kenya and Djibouti never united with independent Somalia. Today, Greater Somalia is represented by both the Somali people still living on ancestral Somali lands and by the stars of the Somali flag, which honor the five territories that make up Somaliweyn (Greater Somalia).

Somali agriculture (particularly livestock and banana exports) and the economy thrived for a short period following Independence, but it didn't take long for dictatorship, regional scrambles for power, and political unrest to lead to the country's eventual collapse and descent into anarchy.

In 1965, Mohamed Siad Barre (Maxamed Siyaad Barre) was appointed the commander in chief of the Somali National Army. In March of 1969, a general election awarded SYL a majority of the seats. In October of 1969, President Abdirashid Ali Shermarke was assassinated by his bodyguard in Laascaanood. On October 21, the day after his burial, General Mohamed Siad Barre led a bloodless military coup and established the Supreme Revolutionary Council.

Somalia then became a state that followed scientific socialism. In 1970, Barre nationalized the major export companies (both Somali and foreign owned) and the banks, as well as the banana plantations. Barre created the National Banana Board, which saw an increase in banana production until the mid-1970s. The creation of the Banana Board came several years after the monopoly the Italians had benefited from via the Royal Banana Monopoly ended in 1963.

The 1970s also brought cooperation agreements between the Soviet Union and Somalia, in which the former supplied weaponry, defense systems, and built air bases and military facilities for Somalia in an attempt to influence the country. Somalia also developed relationships with China and joined the Arab League. Despite these resources, Somalis faced a major drought that decimated the pastoral sector, but they were able to receive aid from several other nations.

In neighboring Ethiopia, a revolution installed a military regime called the Derg in 1974. The United States suspended aid, and the Soviet Union began covertly providing economic assistance to Ethiopia with the hopes of building a red bloc in East Africa. In 1976, the Somali Revolutionary Socialist Party was founded and Siad Barre was elected secretary general. Somalia implemented revolutionary socialist policies like nationalization, a mass literacy and education campaign in rural areas, and free healthcare.

In 1977, alongside the Western Somali Liberation Front, Somali military forces invaded and captured the occupied Ogaden. The Soviet Union and Cuba disapproved of this, and the Somali-Soviet partnership soured. Somalia canceled its cooperation treaty and expelled Soviet advisors. Somalia was seen as the aggressor, alienating both the Soviet Union and the Organization of African Unity (predecessor of the African Union).

The US wanted to limit Soviet influence in the region without publicly supporting Somalia. Somalia and Ethiopia became pawns in the larger Cold War between the US and the Soviet Union. The US covertly supplied Somalia with CIA-backed arms, and in September of 1977, Somalia recaptured Jigjiga, the capital of the Ogaden region, managing to push the war further into Ethiopia. Cuba sent $1 billion and fifteen thousand troops to help Ethiopia reclaim the Ogaden. Facing Cuba, Ethiopia, and the USSR, Somalia lost in 1978 and thousands of Somali refugees fled the region for Somalia.

After the Ogaden War, the US began to offer more public support to Somalia. In 1980, Somalia gave the US access to its Berbera port. In return, in 1983, the US gave Somalia $91 million in military and economic aid and $18 million in aid for refugees. Coming off a failed war and postwar coup attempt, the 1980s mark a decade of agricultural and political decline in Somali history.

While the economy was failing thanks to IMF intervention and devaluation of the Somali shilling, the banana industry was thriving, mostly due to a merger between the state-owned banana producers and the Italian De Nadai group, which led to increased export earnings as well as the privatization and corruption of the banana industry. The increase in banana exports helped offset the loss of livestock exports when Saudi Arabia banned the import of Somali cattle over fears of the rinderpest disease. This ban hit the sector hard—cutting profits from $72 million to $33 million in one year.

Many Somalis soon found themselves at odds with Siad Barre as he spiraled into totalitarianism. Two opposition groups rose to power with Ethiopian financing and support: the Somali National Movement in the north and the Somali Salvation Democratic Front in central Somalia. In response, Barre (who also propped up anti-Derg forces in Ethiopia) silenced, tortured, imprisoned, or killed his critics—particularly those of other clans—further sowing the seeds for a larger societal conflict in the future.

In 1988, the Somali government bombed two cities at the center of the opposition, leading to the razing of Burco and the destruction of 90 percent of Hargeisa. Three hundred thousand people from the Isaaq clan fled to Ethiopia. From 1987 to 1989, Barre killed an estimated two hundred thousand people from the Isaaq clan, with mass graves still being unearthed to this day.

The United States had not only been aware of Barre's actions but actively helped him by delivering arms to the Berbera port and providing PR support to help clean up his image internationally. Barre, who was reliant on that support, felt the loss once the US shifted their attention to the Middle East following the end of the Cold War. This contributed greatly to the further collapse of Somalia. The US then began to express concerns over Barre's human rights violations. In 1990, a large coalition of political, religious, and business groups called for Barre to resign. In January of 1991, the United Somali Congress overthrew Barre, causing widespread violence throughout Mogadishu, the capital city.

On May 18, 1991, Somaliland declared its independence in northwest Somalia. While the Civil War began with the violence against Somaliland, the rest of 1991 would see Mogadishu further engulfed in violence—fracturing the country as a whole and resulting in the deaths of 1 million people, the creation of 2 million refugees abroad, and a Civil War that carried on for years. In this time period, there were many unsuccessful attempts to fill the power vacuum, with opposing clan warlords like Mohamed Farrah Aidid and Ali Mahdi Muhammed violently vying for control in Mogadishu while also battling militia from Siad Barre's clan. This resulted in hundreds of thousands of Somalis being killed or fleeing as refugees. It also deeply impacted agricultural production (particularly grain) and triggered a large-scale famine.

The Civil War had a devastating impact on the economy generally, and in particular, decimated the once thriving banana industry. Banana production ceased and many farmers abandoned their farms, leading to a complete breakdown of the agricultural infrastructure.

Land theft was another issue and farms were taken freely—whether they were abandoned or not—the previous owners never compensated. The new occupants who seized the land after the previous owners left did not have the education or skill set to run these banana farms and later left them in ruins.

From 1992 to 1994, the United States sent troops to Mogadishu to work alongside troops from other nations to restore order before the United Nations arrived to help rebuild the country's infrastructure and distribute food and medicine. However, due to the continuation of the violence, the peacekeeping mission turned into one of "peace enforcement" to the great displeasure of local warlord Mohamed Farrah Aidid. The infamous Battle of Mogadishu took place on October 3 and 4, 1993, between US forces and Somali forces loyal to Aidid, with many US soldiers wounded or killed and hundreds of Somali civilians killed. The battle was considered a great disaster for the US; President Clinton withdrew US troops.

In 1994, banana production restarted, with American Dole-Sombana challenging De Nadai-Somalfruit's monopoly and negotiating exclusive contracts with farmers. Banana production quickly returned to 80 percent of what it was before the war. General Aidid took advantage of this competition between companies by collecting taxes on exports and assuming the power of final approval on contracts with foreign companies. In late 1994, Aidid worked out a deal with Dole guaranteeing a percentage of exports to him and deemed Somalfruit to be "illegal" in late 1994. Soon, he was funding his militia with the $40,000 a week he received from banana profits; Dole-Sombana even purchased a home for Aidid's Somali National Alliance. In 1995, militias representing the companies clashed in a conflict dubbed "the banana wars." This conflict spilled over into the rest of Mogadishu. That same year the UN left Somalia without success in their peacekeeping mission, and Aidid declared himself president. By 1996, he was dead and Dole left Somalia later that year.

In 1997, large-scale flooding in the lower Shabelle led to widespread food instability and loss of income—particularly for those in the agricultural sector. As a result, the banana industry was harmed even further, and by 2002, banana production was limited to regional consumption. Agricultural production shifted toward corn and sesame crops. Additionally, the loss of the export banana business disproportionately impacted many Somali-Bantu people who earned their income from that industry.

In the present day, Somali agricultural and livestock workers face many obstacles. They are vulnerable to climate change, they grapple with high taxation at multiple

checkpoints, crumbling road infrastructure makes product transport difficult, they face security issues, and their products are in heavy competition with foreign imports. It is through agriculture that a clear picture of Somalia's rise and fall in the three decades following independence can be seen.

POST-WAR RECONSTRUCTION

The post-war reconstruction period has been shaped by violence and environmental crises, but it's also marked by rapid redevelopment, attempts at governance, and the rebuilding of Somali society via its economic and agricultural sectors. From 1990 to the early 2000s, there were various attempts at restoring governance in Somalia. In 1998, Puntland, a region in the northeastern part of the country, declared autonomy but not independence from Somalia. In 2004, a transitional government, based in Kenya, was put into place. A parliament was created and Abdullahi Yusuf Ahmed was elected the interim president. Transitional parliament members in exile then began returning to Somalia and met for the first time in 2006.

That same year, the Islamic Courts Union (which became the Supreme Islamic Courts Council) came out in opposition to the transitional government (comprised of the same warlords who terrorized people throughout the previous decade) and took control of southern Somalia. In 2006, Ethiopia sent troops to assist Somali troops (warlord militias) and the transitional government. This intervention led to the killing and displacement of thousands of Somalis in the south at the hands of Ethiopian soldiers. The Supreme Courts Council, then popular, was forced out of Mogadishu by these various troops in 2007. The Council disbanded, but the recently formed terrorist group al-Shabaab (who were the youth militant wing of the Council) remained and began carrying out terror attacks.

From 2009 to 2011, various peacekeeping troops were sent in to help the transitional government; African Union sent in AMISOM, and later Kenyan troops were deployed to Somalia to fight al-Shabaab after the group carried out an attack on their soil. Ethiopian troops exited Somalia, and the parliament elected Sharif Sheikh Ahmed as president and adopted Shari'ah law. There was also a rise in piracy as well as a devastating famine that killed 260,000 people. In the midst of all this, the US began drone warfare in Somalia—which still continues to this day.

In 2012, Hassan Sheikh Mohamud became president, and his government spent the next years fighting al-Shabaab while Somalia experienced rapid redevelopment in part thanks to diaspora returnees who came to rebuild and reinvest. The following decade would bring a visit from US Secretary of State John Kerry, the opening of a Turkish military base, the election of Somali American Mohamed Abdullahi Mohamed "Farmaajo," and Somalia's deadliest al-Shabaab terrorist attack, resulting in the deaths of over five hundred people.

From 2022 to 2024, Hassan Sheikh Mohamud served his second term as president and the country faced a severe drought and flash floods that devastated both agriculture and herding, resulting in 3.5 million livestock dying, the displacement of thousands of people, and food insecurity for millions more.

There were also clashes between Somaliland secessionist troops and local clans in Laascaanood, the capital of the northern Sool region, which is currently contested between Somaliland and Puntland and controlled by pro-Somalia forces. Somaliland and landlocked neighbor Ethiopia signed a memorandum to give Ethiopia sea access, which angered Somalia, who considered this an illegal violation of its sovereignty. In mid-2024, Turkey began mediating the maritime conflict between the two nations. That same year, Somalia and Turkey signed a highly controversial agreement regarding the exploration and production of Somali oil and gas.

Despite everything, the Somalia of the 1990s is not the Somalia that exists now, and that is most evident to the hopeful Somalis, who for three decades kept alive a desire to return home. Today, Somalia is in a state of rapid redevelopment and growth, with many Somalis reinvesting in the infrastructure and economy of the country. With this rapid development linger security and governance issues, corruption, foreign influence and intervention, and an economy in flux. Still, regardless of its many challenges, Somalia is undoubtedly a nation in the process of rebirth.

SOMALI CUISINE IN WRITING AND AROUND THE WORLD

For Somalis, words are deeply meaningful. They tell us who we are as a people, and they hold stories of our ancestors and ourselves. The Soomaali language was not rendered in Latin characters until 1972. Prior to that, several local scripts were used, including Osmanya, but the Somali spoken-word tradition reaches back many centuries. We documented everything through spoken word, passing down stories, songs, and history, as well as the poetry that is such an integral part of Somali cultural identity, so much so that Somalia is globally known as a Nation of Poets.

Starting in 1974, the Somali government initiated a mass literacy campaign that sought to bring written af Soomaali to every corner of the country. Because the possibility of writing and publishing in Somali is so recent, there are few published Somali cookbooks or other written resources on Somali cuisine even today. A notable exception to this is Asha Mohamud Guled's 1978 *A Cookery of Somali Style* (*Habka Cunto-Karinta Soomaaliyeed*). The first of its kind, this cookbook documents traditional and modern Somali recipes, from rice, meat, and vegetable dishes to drinks and sweets. It also serves as a primer on Somali history, people, geography, language, and the role of Somali women. Guled wrote the book for a Somali embassy fundraiser in Washington, DC, and, according to Somali writer and researcher Ibrahim Hirsi, her effort was supported by a Somali government deeply interest in promoting Somali language, literacy, and culture.

There would not be another major Somali cookbook for nearly another thirty years, when Barlin Ali, a Somali American woman, published *Somali Cuisine* in 2007. By this time, the Somali Civil War had been ongoing for years, and the Somali diaspora had spread across the globe. *Somali Cuisine* is so much more than just a cookbook—it's a physical representation of culinary knowledge passed down by, and among, Somali women. (And though it shares traditional recipes, it's also clearly informed by Ali's migration to the United States.)

If *A Cookery of Somali Style* and *Somali Cuisine* were the pioneering Somali cookbooks, *Xawaash* was a pioneering website. Ontario-based couple Leila Adde and Abdullahi Kassim are the masterminds behind the internationally popular food blog founded in 2011, with a mission of carrying on the work of preserving Somali cuisine (see page 58). While Asha Mohamud Guled and Barlin Ali transferred orally transmitted recipes to print, Adde and Kassim preserved them digitally, publishing them for the diaspora of online Somali communities popping up alongside the geographical diaspora.

In 2018, another cookbook, *Soo Fariista—Come Sit Down*, was published. This book was the collective effort of Somali American students who shared seventy traditional recipes, interviewed family members, and shared stories of their various journeys to resettlement in the United States—an effort to preserve Somali foodways and share their own personal migration stories. It's the first Somali cookbook written by a collective, which feels like an appropriate continuation of the way Somali culinary knowledge has long been shared.

SOMALI RESTAURANTS

Halal stores are the heartbeat of Somali diasporic communities, and Somali restaurants are the soul. For many immigrant communities, restaurants serve as a familiar home base in their newly adopted countries. In these culinary spaces, immigrants can experience a sense of safety and belonging that is in sharp contrast to the ways they might normally feel othered in their new homes.

Some of the earliest Somali restaurants and cafés abroad were in England, where Somali sailors began to settle in the 1920s. These single seamen, particularly from the British protectorate of Somaliland, were recruited as cheap labor on British vessels. Some Somali seamen began to set up boarding houses in England to meet the demand for housing. Many of their fellow countrymen experienced racial discrimination and had a difficult time securing places to stay, particularly while they were on short periods of leave.

Ali Mohamed Elmi, a Somali sailor, recounts a cousin settling in England in 1928 and opening up a restaurant. He also describes living in a Somali boarding house at some point that had a café on the premises catering to young Somali seamen in East London, of which there were many. These spaces were necessary given the lack of dining options for seamen during their voyages. Meanwhile, across the pond, Somali sailors fresh off Italian cargo ships landed in New York in 1900, first settling in the Bowery neighborhood before eventually making Harlem their home. By the 1950s, the community had grown, housing delis, community centers, and Somali cafés, such as one that stood in the location that has hosted Safari, the only remaining Somali restaurant in New York, since 2016.

It is not a surprise that seafaring Somali men would seek out the nearest Somali café or restaurant in early twentieth-century Britain or mid-twentieth-century New York.

This desire to find a community, *your people*, as a recent arrival, is a hallmark of the diasporic experience.

Nearly four years ago, I found myself in the city of Chicago for the first time, for a friend's wedding. I did what I always do when I am in a new place: I looked up the nearest Somali restaurant. I was surprised to find several, so I opted to go to the nearest one for lunch. As soon as I spotted the restaurant, I noticed dozens of cabs parked just outside.

When I went inside, I realized this particular restaurant was a hub for local Somali cabbies, who would drop by between rides to grab some shaah, a quick bite, or to spend time with their fellow countrymen. I found myself greatly comforted by this and grateful that I was welcomed and could experience my community, even in a city I had never been to before. It's clear that the desire for belonging and the need to find community hasn't really changed, whether it's Somali sailors in search of it in 1920s English port towns or Somali cab drivers in Chicago in the twenty-first century.

Somali restaurants in the diaspora serve as a type of informal culinary diplomacy and an opportunity for cultural exchange. Unlike countries like Thailand, Spain, or South Korea that embark on formal government-supported endeavors of gastrodiplomacy, there is no funding from the Somali national government to spread or promote Somali cuisine globally.

Where there have been Somali people, there have almost always been Somali eateries. When Somali restaurants exist abroad, it is often because they are there to serve the people in that area. They also largely serve classic Somali food, even as restaurants in Somalia experiment and move Somali culinary traditions forward. Due to the function they serve in Somali communities, restaurants abroad remain frozen in time, serving classic dishes to a nostalgic and often homesick diaspora.

Perhaps it is because they exist for Somali people that Somali restaurants are infamous for not advertising to non-Somalis. One would think this might be at odds with the importance Somali culture places on hospitality, but instead it's an indication of how insular Somali communities can be and how steadfast we have been in resisting assimilation in favor of maintaining our strong cultural identity.

When I was growing up in Seattle in the early 2000s, there was a local (now demolished) restaurant called Marwa that was a simple, no-frills Somali restaurant established to meet the needs of a growing Somali population. Marwa was located in Tukwila, a suburb south of Seattle. Many Somali families (including my own) had initially been resettled in Tukwila upon our arrivals to the United States.

Marwa became our neighborhood restaurant, and it was the Somali restaurant that my family first frequented upon our resettlement in America. Having a restaurant like Marwa in our new city signified that we could perhaps belong. We went there for Eid celebrations, special occasions, or just to enjoy a meal out. When we weren't at Marwa, we were shopping at the adjoining halal market for our beloved Somali foods.

For my mother, who survived a war and had to restart her entire life in a new country with young children in tow, I'm sure Marwa and the adjoining businesses felt like a lifeline and the closest thing to home.

Today, eateries like Banadir in Los Angeles, Sabiib in London, Safari in New York, and Xawaash in Toronto are Somali restaurants catering to the second and third generations of Somalis in Canada, Europe, and the United States. Their existence is proof of the lasting importance of Somali restaurants when it comes to the preservation of Somali identity in the diaspora, one hundred years out from the establishment of those first Somali cafés in England.

CHAPTER 2

THE SOMALI PANTRY

The beginning of the Somali Civil War, in 1991, sparked a mass exodus of Somalis to all corners of the planet. This was the largest-ever migration of Somalis out of the country, resulting in an estimated 2 million Somalis now living outside of Somalia.

Throughout the Somali diaspora, from Seattle to Stockholm, certain core ingredients are found in Somali households. This chapter explores these building blocks of Somali cuisine. While it's not necessary to have all these ingredients on hand to make the recipes in this book, building a Somali pantry will make it easier—and will give you a deeper understanding of the flavors that characterize Somali cuisine.

SPICES AND HERBS

Somalia was known to the ancient Greeks as Aromata, or the Cape of Spices, and its history of international trade dates back many centuries. The port of Mogadishu is at least a thousand years old. In ancient and medieval times, traders from India, China, the Middle East, and Europe would pass through Somali ports, trading goods with locals. Somalia was a place of great wealth—of gold, livestock, frankincense, myrrh, and spices.

When Moroccan traveler Ibn Battuta visited Mogadishu in 1331, he described a town of "enormous size, inhabited by merchants with vast resources," with a textile industry that exported fabrics to Egypt and Jerusalem. In the words of Somali archivist Qaman Omar, Somalia has always been "a corridor between the East and the West."

These centuries of far-flung trade brought diverse spices and flavors to Somali cuisine. Xawaash, the main spice mix used in Somali food, is a warming blend that makes our cuisine taste distinctly *Somali*. Seven whole spices (cumin, coriander, black pepper, cinnamon, cardamom, cloves, and turmeric) are toasted until fragrant and then ground to a smooth golden-brown powder (see page 56). This evocative mix will have your house smelling like a traditional Somali home.

The spices and herbs most common in Somali cooking include cardamom, cumin, coriander, fennel seed, ginger, turmeric, cinnamon, cloves, paprika, black pepper, curry powder, cilantro, and basil. Two imported products, Maggi chicken bouillon cubes and Vegeta seasoning mix, are now also kitchen staples, and you will find them listed in some of the recipes in this book.

FRUITS AND VEGETABLES

The Somali climate varies regionally, but the vegetables and fruits Somalis eat are typically ones that grow well in warm and tropical climates. There is one fruit that is totally central to Somali cuisine, more so than others, but the Somali diet includes dates, coconut, mango, melon, grapes, lemon, lime, apples, tamarind, strawberries, watermelon, papaya, figs, guava (saytuun), soursop (canuuni), pear (cambaruud), golden apple (isbaandhees), hohob (grewia asiatica), pomegranate (ruman), quince (qoonne), jujube (gob), grapefruit (bambeelmo), avocado (afakaadho), murcood (yellow plum), mareer (cordia dichotoma), and dhafaruur (grewia tenax), among others. Vegetables central to Somali cooking include tomatoes, okra, onions, cucumbers, garlic, spinach, Swiss chard, radishes, potatoes, sweet potatoes, pumpkin, corn, chiles, peppers, eggplant, carrot, lettuce, zucchini, cassava, and cabbage.

The fruit that is so fundamental that even non-Somalis understand we pair it with almost everything is the humble banana—this even though the mass production of bananas only started in southern Somalia as a cash crop (by Italian colonists) in the 1920s. But before long, Somali bananas were known to be "unmatched in taste and texture," in the words of agricultural engineer Edward Baars. By 1990, just one year shy of the Somali Civil War, Somalia was the largest African exporter of bananas to Europe and the Middle East, and the banana trade was worth $96 million, an all-time high.

This industry was, of course, decimated during the war. Today, it is working to make a comeback, with banana farmers gradually returning to the farms that have been in their families for generations. Fruit conglomerate Del Monte has also begun banana production at a farm in Somaliland.

GRAINS AND LEGUMES

Pasta (another relic of Italian colonialism) and rice are the starchy backbones of most modern Somali dishes, including both vegetarian dishes and those that include meat. Pasta is often served with variations of tomato suugo (sauce); both rice and pasta are often accompanied by sides of basbaas (hot sauce), salad, and a banana.

Corn, sorghum, and millet also play crucial roles in the Somali diet. Corn flour and cornmeal are used in muufo, a corn flatbread, and soor, a polenta-like dish served with stews and soups or mixed with buttermilk and sugar. Sorghum and corn are the base of canjeero, the sour fermented pancake that is a staple of Somali cuisine. Adzuki beans appear on the table as cambuulo, a sweet bean dish that can be eaten with rice or dusted with sugar and a little sesame oil.

In Islamic medicine, ground nigella seeds have deeply healing properties, and many Somali families eat them to help strengthen their immune systems. Other staples include wheat, barley, lentils, mung beans, sesame seeds, yicib, and black-eyed peas.

MEAT, POULTRY, AND SEAFOOD

The modern Somali diet prioritizes meat, eggs, milk, and starch-based foods like pasta and rice, (the pasta in particular is a departure from the indigenous Somali diet). There is a commonly held belief among Somalis that if one's meal doesn't include meat, one hasn't really eaten, and while goat, lamb, beef, and chicken are staple meats, the most coveted meat is camel meat. Traditionally, many Somalis were nomadic pastoralists, and camel herding has been a way of life for many, many generations (see page 136). Not only is Somalia a country with many camels, but the care for and appreciation of camels in Somali culture runs deep; poetry is written about this beloved animal. Beyond their use as food and for transportation, camels have also served as a form of currency and an indicator of wealth and position in Somali society. For Somalis abroad, camel meat can be a hard-to-source delicacy—often needing to be flown in from countries like Australia, and, when it can be found, at a local halal grocer (see page 196).

Although Somalia has the longest coastline in mainland Africa, seafood dishes are mostly limited to Somalis who live in coastal fishing towns. Everywhere else, red meat is preferred. Somalis in the diaspora often rely on canned tuna or firm white fish and salmon for their home cooking.

DAIRY AND OILS

Like meat, milk is one of the most important foods in Somali culture, and many parents prioritize their children's milk consumption. Just like camel meat, camel's milk is prized and is believed to have many health benefits. While the camel is king, Somalis also drink cow's milk and goat's milk (including buttermilks of each).

Ghee, also known as subag, is a coveted form of dairy. It goes into everything from desserts to savory rice-and-meat dishes. For breakfast, it's spooned on top of canjeero (the traditional Somali pancake) that is then soaked in sweet shaah (spiced tea). Cow's milk ghee is most common, but Somalis also use goat's milk ghee.

Other dairy and oil pantry staples include olive oil, vegetable oil, coconut oil, and sesame oil. Among these, sesame oil is an incredibly popular addition to many Somali dishes, from goat soup and muufo to cambuulo (adzuki beans) topped with sesame oil and sugar.

TOOLS

The Somali kitchen does not require many specialty tools. A good blender will be essential, as well as both a mortar and pestle and a flat crepe or canjeero pan. One specialty tool that does exist is a coconut grating chair which is often found throughout East Africa. Somali cooks have long used various heat sources and equipment, such as a burjiko or traditional portable charcoal stove and a tinaar (tandoor oven) to make flatbreads. Some dishes are prepared in a traditional clay pot called a dheri. Fire and pit cooking is also another method for making food. Although these cooking options give distinct flavors and textures to foods, standard stoves and ovens will work just as well. While it does not count as a cooking tool, it is customary to burn uunsi (frankincense and myrrh incense) after cooking a meal or before receiving guests.

A NOTE ON SALT

Somali recipes use several means to achieve salty flavor: Maggi chicken bouillon cubes, Vegeta seasoning, and salt. The first two of these are European products that have become absolute staples in Somali cooking; they are easy to find online and in many specialty stores. The recipes in this book use ordinary table salt, unless fine sea salt or another salt is specified.

SUUQA: THE MARKET

In Somali households across the globe, the tasks of grocery shopping and cooking are largely the responsibility of the women and girls. Asha Mohamed Guled—the author of the very first Somali cookbook published in English, *A Cookery of Somali Style* (1978)—dedicates her book to "the women of Somalia in participation [*sic*] of their love and concern for every aspect of their family's care."

While there are Somali men who can and do cook at home, some elders consider it ceeb (shameful) to find a man in the kitchen, and this belief is often still held across the diaspora. However, this doesn't necessarily apply to Somali restaurants, where one is in fact more likely to find a man doing the cooking, mirroring the larger gender dynamic in the restaurant world, where male chefs dominate.

Back home in Somalia, food shopping, meal preparation, and cooking are all daily rituals. Food is not an afterthought but a part of the diurnal rhythms of each household. It's common for grocery shopping to be done each day, the fresh vegetables or fruits needed for the day's meals bought at local markets or sidewalk produce stands. Grocery shopping is not only about buying food; it also serves as a form of community building. Women doing their shopping have relationships with the vendors they see every day, and these exchanges support the local economy directly. The act of baking bread is also communal in Somalia, where people can take their homemade dough to a local bakery and use the bakery's oven.

This form of community extends beyond grocery shopping; it reflects the function that making and eating food serves within Somali society. When meals are made at home, it's not uncommon for friends, neighbors, or extended family to just drop by. In fact, it's expected, and regardless of how much or how little food one has, it is

an important aspect of Somali culture to break bread with anyone who comes to your home. Hospitality is ingrained deeply into Somali culture, so this norm applies wherever Somalis are found.

However, this hyperlocal way of shopping for and consuming fresh food daily has shifted significantly as Somalis have migrated globally post–Civil War. Somali women and girls still carry the gendered responsibility of nourishing their households while also working outside of the home or attending school. Somalis who have resettled in Europe, North America, and Australia, where the climates and cultures are vastly different, have had to adapt their shopping habits. Not only is it harder to find the ingredients they're accustomed to, but even familiar foods in newly adopted countries often don't taste the same. In a study published on Somali women's experiences of cooking and meals after immigrating to Sweden, a participant stated, "The bananas here have no taste."

Produce tasting different is something I've experienced in my own travels to Somalia. The daily shopping that Somalis are accustomed to back home makes for the freshest of ingredients: fish caught that morning along Somalia's extensive coast, freshly harvested vegetables and fruits brought to the markets by local farmers, and still-warm cakes bought from a doolsho (cake) lady or a bakery in the neighborhood.

Cooking and sharing food as a form of community building is also different for Somalis abroad. While new kitchen tools, frozen meals, and expedited cooking processes provide some convenience, these can't replace what's been lost. The routine of families eating meals together; a culture of regularly interacting with neighbors, or welcoming them with food; and even the expectation of Fridays as the Islamic day dedicated to community and worship—all of these have changed.

The attitudes of Somali kids growing up in the diaspora toward their traditional foods have also transformed. A study of the eating habits of members of the Somali community in Sweden found that many parents feel pressured by their children to feed them Western-style foods because they're uninterested in eating (or learning to make) Somali foods.

Where traditional ingredients can still be found, it's thanks to the establishment of Somali-owned halal stores in the new diasporic communities. These stores are the heartbeat of Somali communities abroad and the closest thing to the suuqs many grew up with in Somalia. It's here that Somalis can buy halal meats, sweets, spices to make xawaash, fruit juices, and—before the rise of WhatsApp—phone cards so they could speak to relatives long-distance.

These halal stores are also hubs of information and community, where newly arrived people can find resources, produce, and establish relationships with other Somalis. In 2003, my hooyo opened up one of these markets in Seattle. Hamdi Market, in the north Seattle neighborhood of Lake City, was named for my baby sister and run by my mother until she sold it in 2006.

Somalis began to first settle in Seattle in the 1970s and 1980s as small numbers of college students and professionals came to the city. However, large waves of Somali refugees began arriving in Seattle in the mid-to-late 1990s. My family was on the early side of this mass migration, arriving in Seattle in 1996. By the time my mother opened Hamdi Market, the community had grown exponentially and the need for such halal stores was clear. Hamdi Market became a place for the Somalis in north Seattle to get their meat and their rugs, to send money back home, and to stop in for a cup of shaah iyo sheeko (tea and conversation). My mother recognized the need—that small stores like these would be at the heart of our communities. Intentionally or not, they re-created some of the comforts and traditions that Somalis had known back home and helped bring along what was left behind.

Today, most post-war Somali diasporic communities in Western countries are at least thirty years old. In Minneapolis, which has one of the largest Somali populations outside of Somalia, one can even find specialty ingredients in larger, more mainstream stores. When stocking your own Somali pantry, you can usually find the fruits and vegetables you need at any grocery store. When a recipe calls for a specialty food, first check to see if your city has a Somali population and a Somali-owned halal store. These stores are most likely to carry Somali brands. For ingredients like basmati rice, spices, ghee, or oils, any Middle Eastern, African, or South Asian market or grocery store should work. For meats, such stores may suffice if you can't find a local halal butcher. It should be relatively simple to stock your pantry from any of these places, setting yourself up to successfully prepare, share, and enjoy Somali food.

0,39,66

CHAPTER 3

Condiments

It's no exaggeration to say that xawaash is at the heart of Somali cuisine. It is Somali history on a plate—a culinary reminder of Somalia's centuries of global trade, particularly along the Indian Ocean. Xawaash is what makes many Somali dishes taste distinctly *Somali.* While every household's xawaash recipe is its own, typically seven core spices—cumin, coriander, black pepper, cinnamon, cardamom, cloves, and turmeric—are toasted until their fragrance blooms, then blended into an earthy golden-brown powder. Xawaash stores very well and for a long time in an airtight container, though it's at its peak shortly after it's made. If you use it often (and many recipes in this book call for it), you can double or triple the recipe for a big batch.

Xawaash *(SOMALI SPICE MIX)*

MAKES ABOUT 2½ CUPS (260 G)

- 1 cup (100 g) whole cumin seeds
- 1 cup (70 g) whole coriander seeds
- ¼ cup (35 g) black peppercorns
- 1 small-to-medium piece of cinnamon bark
- 2 tablespoons green cardamom pods
- 1½ teaspoons whole cloves
- ¼ cup (30 g) ground turmeric

Toast the cumin, coriander, peppercorns, cinnamon bark, cardamom pods, and cloves in a medium skillet over medium heat, stirring constantly so the spices don't burn. The spices are toasted when they have a slightly darker color and become fragrant, 1 to 2 minutes.

Transfer the toasted spices to a blender or spice grinder and blend until they become a fine powder. Transfer to a bowl and mix in the ground turmeric until it's fully incorporated and the spice mix is golden brown. Allow to cool completely, then store in an airtight container.

> The most common Somali condiments are various basbaas (hot sauces), varying from region to region, that accompany rice- and meat-based dishes. However, arguably the most important ingredient in Somali cuisine is xawaash, a seven-spice mix that is the anchoring flavor of many Somali dishes. That said, Somali cuisine is diverse enough that it's possible for a person to have never tried a particular dish if it's not from their region. In the diaspora, there is a general sense of what Somali cuisine is, and it doesn't always include regional condiments, like the mango and tamarind chutney called leeleefow (page 75), for example. Aside from xawaash and subag (ghee), which serve as the flavor bases for many dishes, condiments are always offered on the side.

XAWAASH, THE BLOG

The written recipe is a fairly new phenomenon in the span of human history, and it's even more recent for Somalis than for people in other parts of the world. For thousands of years, our living oral tradition has archived our recipes in the same manner that we preserve our poetry and our stories. So what happens when knowledge is no longer passed down orally? When it leaves the tongue of one generation but has difficulty making it to the ear of the next?

For more than a generation of Somalis in the diaspora, this cultural transmission has been interrupted—first by the Civil War that began in 1991, then by the resulting mass international migration. Like a dropped phone call, much knowledge that was meant to be transferred from one generation to another has been lost.

Millennials in the Somali diaspora have been able to reconnect with our cultural knowledge thanks, in many ways, to the internet. In the early 2010s, when blogs were a cultural phenomenon and many young Somalis were getting online, diasporic internet communities started popping up. The transfer of cultural knowledge and resources began to become digitized. Pioneers included Xawaash, the food blog that taught a generation of Somali diaspora kids on the internet how to cook.

Xawaash was founded in 2011 by Leila Adde and Abdullahi Kassim, a married couple who grew up in Somalia and eventually resettled in Kitchener, Ontario. The self-described "food-loving" pair, who were running a secondhand clothing export business, decided to start a food blog in their downtime. On weekends in Kitchener, their home would be filled with the sounds of oud-heavy Somali music and as many as sixty friends and family members, all feasting on dishes they had prepared. "It was good practice. . . . We used to try out different recipes," Kassim recalls.

They collected recipes from their parents and from relatives all over the world, from Australia to Kenya, preserving unique regional Bravanese (Barawani) and Somali recipes like kalamuudo (page 165) and bariis isku karis (page 173) before the older generation passed on.

While Xawaash wasn't the only Somali food blog on the scene, it had a lasting impact. Adde and Kassim not only thoughtfully created a digital archive of recipes, like soor iyo maraq and oodkac, that were formerly passed down only orally, they also connected a whole generation to this culinary legacy, preserving knowledge and effectively rebuilding the cultural transmission of our recipes.

Almost immediately, Adde and Kassim's blog became a hit, finding its way to every corner of the global Somali diaspora. Its audience continued to grow as they added recipe videos to the blog as well as instructions in Somali, English, and Arabic. But Xawaash's popularity really exploded when the bloggers started a YouTube channel. For older Somalis, YouTube was a way to keep up with politics and their peers around the globe or to nostalgically revisit all the things from their youth that the war had destroyed and that now lived only online—like old ruwaayad (theater) performances and concerts or footage of Somali cities as they once stood.

For a younger generation who had never experienced their parents' Somalia, YouTube provided a window to the past, showcasing prewar Somalia and its golden age of art, music, and cultural production. It was here that Xawaash found another audience: viewers from Adde and Kassim's generation who no longer had to deal with language barriers or learning how to access the blog—they could simply watch. The results speak for themselves: 199,000 subscribers, millions of views, and thousands of comments. "Thank you so much for all the recipes. I grew up in America, and I didn't learn how to cook anything. I was made fun of all the time for burning and making bad food. Now that I have you guys, I can make anything. Truly, thank you," reads one reply to a video about samosa wraps.

Xawaash also found its younger millennial audience via the popular 2010s microblogging site Tumblr. On Tumblr, young Somalis formed a community and made friendships with other Somali millennials living thousands of miles away; many of these connections between "Reer Tumblr" (a.k.a. Tumblr family) are still going strong today. On Tumblr, Somalis reposted recipes as well as Xawaash's iconic spice map: each ingredient of Somalia's famous xawaash spice mix laid out in the geographic shape of the country, featuring golden turmeric and chunks of cinnamon bark nestled near a horn of coriander seed and earthy green cardamom pods. For many, it was their first time seeing Somali cuisine represented on the internet.

For others, Xawaash became both a guide and a cultural lifeline. "If only you could see the types of things people said when they wrote to us," Kassim says, laughing, as he recounted how many emails and comments he and Adde had received through the years. "There were Somali students studying in Turkey who told us they entered an 'ethnic food' competition and came out on top because of Xawaash. Once a girl wrote to us from China saying we had saved her marriage."

Xawaash's impact is still evident today. "I've loved Xawaash since I was a teenager, when I first got into cooking. I would look up recipes because my mom didn't have her recipes written down," says Los Angeles–based filmmaker and model Miski Muse. "It's still the number one place I go to for Somali recipes to this day, and I even use it when I throw dinner parties or if I'm feeling nostalgic." Writer Jamila Osman remembers eating an incredible date cake at Xawaash restaurant in Toronto and searching for something similar upon her return home to Portland, Oregon; she found the recipe on Xawaash.

For Somali chefs and recipe developers like me, who have to translate oral recipes into written ones, Xawaash has served as a helpful guide when, for example, I've needed to translate my family's abstract forms of measurement into something others can utilize, or to provide context about the history of a dish. It has often been one of the only culinary resources available to me, outside of learning from my elders in person.

Considering the lack of representation and knowledge of Somali cuisine in the mainstream, Xawaash has served as a primary source on Somali cuisine for non-Somalis as well. For Ohio-based archivist Qaman Omar, Xawaash also offered something more meaningful than just recipes: positive representation. "Xawaash, for me and my mom, was less a recipe resource and more a kind of digital museum of Somali cookery and its interpretations. We marveled at seeing our traditional foods committed to the digital space in a time when nearly all media about Somali people and culture was negative."

As Xawaash's influence grew over the years, supporters of the blog encouraged Adde and Kassim to open their own restaurant. Kassim would answer jokingly that they would only open a restaurant if they "had a million dollars." After years of cajoling—and upon realizing that their clothing business of nearly ten years was no longer viable—Adde and Kassim opened Xawaash the restaurant in Toronto in 2015, eventually turning their effort from their blog and YouTube channel to the restaurant. Xawaash's international online support created a customer base who flocked to the restaurant to eat dishes like chicken mandi and rice or braised lamb, eventually allowing Adde and Kassim to open a second location, in Mississauga, in 2019.

When I ask if he ever expected that the blog he and Leila started as an archival side project would not only lead to a restaurant empire but help so many Somalis in the diaspora connect with their culinary and cultural roots, Abdullahi replies, "We never imagined this would happen in our wildest of dreams."

Like Somali women throughout history, I first learned to cook from my mother, who learned from her mother, who learned from hers. But many of my peers in the diaspora learned to cook from the internet. One is an oral tradition, the other a digital one—but both allow us to preserve and share our culture. The latter was made possible for an entire generation thanks to pioneers like Xawaash.

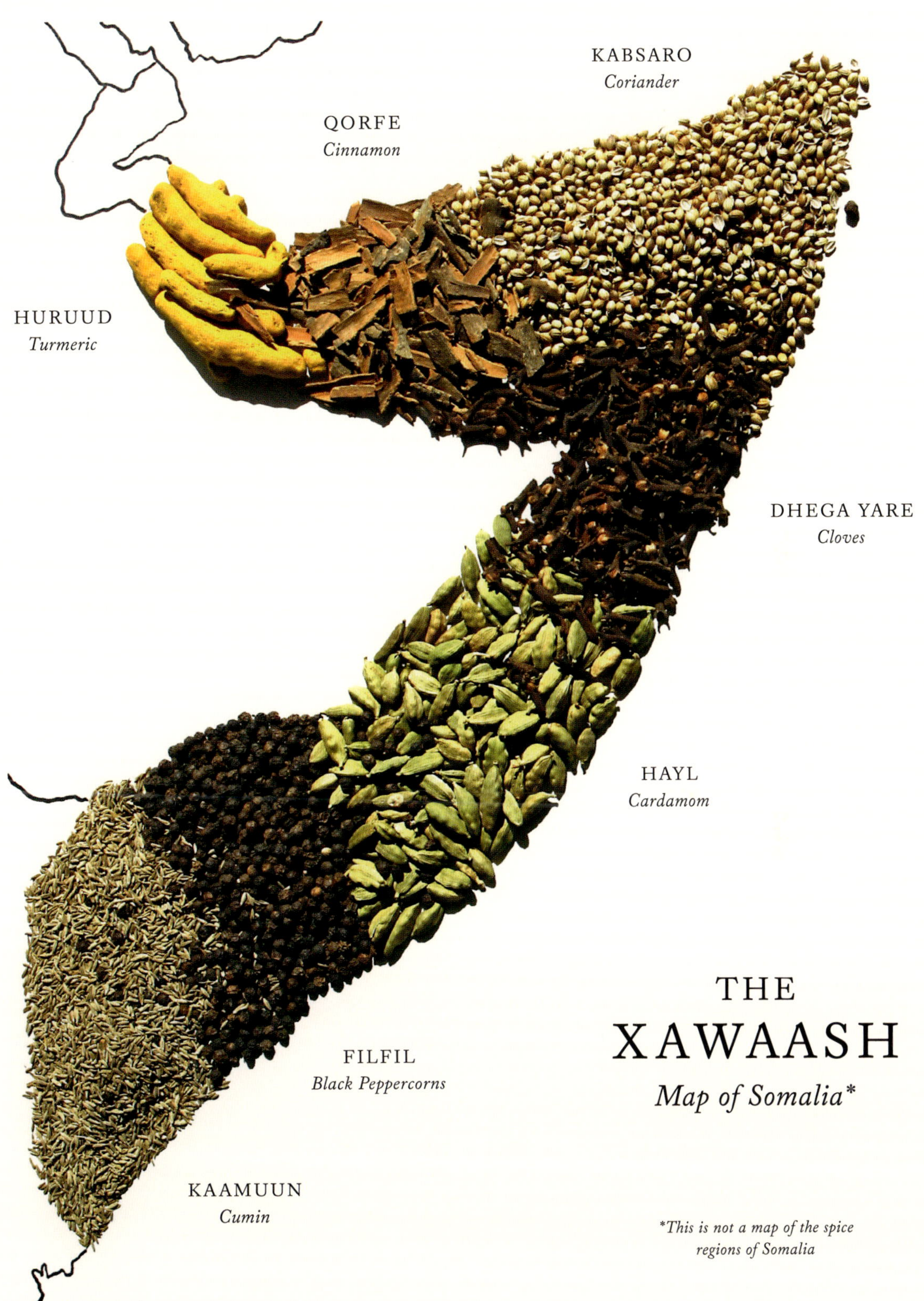

THE XAWAASH

*Map of Somalia**

**This is not a map of the spice regions of Somalia*

While spices play an integral role in Somali cuisine, Somali food is not overly spicy-hot. Basbaas (hot sauce) is, however, a spicy condiment that accompanies most main dishes—offered on the side for those who want it. The heat of basbaas is usually balanced by the creamy sweetness of bananas served alongside. This vibrant green blended basbaas marries heat with garlic and salty lemon, complementing a dish rather than overtaking it. If a milder heat is preferred, de-seed the peppers. Basbaas is best eaten when it's first made, as it loses its kick over time.

Basbaas Cagaaroo la Shiiday *(BLENDED GREEN HOT SAUCE)*

MAKES ABOUT 1¼ CUPS (300 ML)

3 large jalapeño chiles, coarsely chopped

1 small serrano chile, coarsely chopped

½ cup (8 g) loosely packed chopped cilantro leaves and stems

4 large garlic cloves, peeled

½ small red onion, coarsely chopped

¼ cup (60 ml) distilled white vinegar

Juice of 1 large lemon (about ¼ cup / 60 ml)

1¼ teaspoons fine sea salt

In a blender, combine all the ingredients and blend until smooth. Store in an airtight container in the fridge for up to a week.

This basbaas has very similar ingredients to the blended basbaas on page 63, but its texture is very different: The pounded garlic and chiles offer a stronger flavor profile, and the chunky consistency complements seafood and meat dishes, offering more concentrated bites of heat than the uniform heat of a blended basbaas. A mortar and pestle is the ideal tool for making this basbaas: Pound the garlic and chiles directly in the mortar, then mix in all the liquids. This basbaas will separate as it sits, so mix it with a spoon before serving.

Basbaas Cagaaroo la Tumay *(POUNDED GREEN HOT SAUCE)*

MAKES ABOUT 1 CUP (240 ML)

12 large (45 g) garlic cloves, peeled

⅓ cup (5 g) cilantro leaves, very finely chopped (optional)

1¾ ounces (50 g) fresh large green Thai chiles (about 13), chopped

Juice of 2 limes

7 tablespoons (100 ml) distilled white vinegar

1¼ teaspoon fine sea salt

Pound the garlic in a mortar and pestle until all the cloves are broken up, then add the cilantro and pound until the cilantro and garlic form a thick pulp. Add the chopped chiles and pound until they break down into a chunky pulp.

Add the lime juice, vinegar, and salt. Stir all the ingredients together and serve, or store in an airtight container in the fridge for up to 3 days.

OYALFORD
JUMBO

Tamarind is a common ingredient in Somali cuisine and is frequently found in meat dishes, basbaas, and rice dishes. Its distinct flavor serves as the base of this basbaas, which gets its reddish-brown color from both tamarind and tomatoes. The sweet-and-sour flavor of the tamarind also weaves beautifully with the heat of the peppers. Use a seedless tamarind paste and soak it first for easier blending (see below). Store the basbaas in an airtight container in the fridge for up to a week and mix to blend before using (it may separate). Basbaas raqay pairs beautifully with sambuus (pages 106, 110) or nafaqo (page 112) and makes an excellent gift for friends and family alike.

Basbaas Raqay *(TAMARIND HOT SAUCE)*

MAKES 5½ CUPS (1.3 L)

3 cups (720 ml) room-temperature water

7½ ounces (210 g) seedless tamarind paste

½ cup plus 1 tablespoon (55 g) Vegeta seasoning (see page 48)

½ medium red onion, chopped

8 ounces (225 g) serrano chiles, chopped

2 medium tomatoes, cored and quartered

15 garlic cloves, peeled

Juice of 3 limes

½ medium green bell pepper, chopped

1 tablespoon salt

Combine the water and tamarind paste in a medium bowl and let soak for 10 minutes.

Pour the tamarind and its liquid into a blender and add the Vegeta, onion, chiles, tomatoes, garlic, lime juice, bell pepper, and salt. Purée to a smooth consistency. Serve or refrigerate, tightly covered, for up to a week.

Liimo ajaar is a lemon pickle condiment that is largely eaten in southern Somalia and particularly associated with Somalis from the community in Baraawe, Somalia. This ajaar has many similarities to lemon achaar that is consumed in Indian culinary traditions. Liimo ajaar can be made with lemons or limes and is left to pickle in its own juices. Liimo ajaar is tart, salty, and spicy—although spice levels are adjusted according to one's own preference. It is customary to pickle the lemon with lemon juice and to quarter it without cutting the lemon fully. However, to make a quicker pickle, some slice the lemons thinner or use a method of boiling the lemons in hot water before beginning the pickling process. While only lemon juice is used here, some people also use vinegar, although that preparation is less common. The peppers are spicy, so do make sure to wear gloves when cutting them. Serve with any rice and meat dishes or with pasta dishes like kalamuudo (page 165). The ajaar is left undisturbed in a warm place for several weeks, but once it's opened, make sure to store it in the fridge.

Liimo Ajaar *(LEMON PICKLE)*

MAKES 4 CUPS (800 ML)

5 large lemons

2 tablespoons ground turmeric

2 tablespoons fine sea salt

13 green Thai chiles (40 g)

3 red chiles (35 g)

1 cup (230 ml) lemon juice

Wash and clean the lemons and cut off the very ends. Quarter the lemons, place in a large bowl, and mix in the turmeric and 1 tablespoon of the salt.

In a blender, combine the green and red chile peppers, ½ cup of the lemon juice, and the remaining 1 tablespoon salt and blend until smooth. Add the hot sauce mixture to the bowl and mix together until the lemons are covered.

Transfer the lemons and the liquid to a large glass jar and cover with the remaining ½ cup lemon juice. Close the jar and leave it out at room temperature for 3 or 4 days. Next, open the jar to "burp" it from the fizzy gas build up. Close the jar and keep it in a room temperature place for the remaining 21 days. Enjoy with foods such as kalamuudo. Store the container in the fridge once it's been opened.

Shidni, also known as shigni, is a spicy tamarind chutney; the addition of dates gives this basbaas a slightly sweet flavor that balances the heat of the peppers and the tartness of the tamarind. Enjoy with meats, seafood, or rice.

Shidni *(TAMARIND CHUTNEY)*

MAKES ABOUT 3 CUPS (720 ML)

3 large Medjool dates, pitted

2 medium tomatoes, chopped

7 garlic cloves, peeled

10 fresh green Thai chiles

⅓ cup (80 ml) vegetable oil

¼ red onion, quartered

2 ounces (60 g) seedless tamarind paste

⅔ cup (10 g) cilantro leaves and tender stems

1⅔ cups (400 ml) water

5 ounces (140 g) tomato paste

1 teaspoon salt

Combine all the ingredients in a blender and purée until smooth.

In a medium pot over medium heat, cook the puréed shidni, covered, for 1 hour, stirring occasionally. When the shidni is thickened, with small pools of oil floating to the top, remove from the heat and let cool to room temperature. Store it in an airtight container in the fridge; it will keep for 7 days.

Coconuts grow all around Somalia and are used in both sweet dishes like kashaato and savory ones like this basbaas. This coconut basbaas can be found across southern Somalia, where it's a staple, especially in the homes of the Reer Xamar community. Fresh coconut would normally be used, but this recipe calls for dried shredded coconut, which is a substitution many in the diaspora have adopted. The dried coconut is hydrated before being blended into the rest of the ingredients. The texture of this basbaas varies by personal preference—some blend it very smoothly and some prefer a half chunky, half smooth texture. Some in the diaspora also add mayonnaise. Mix before serving to avoid separation and store in an airtight container in the fridge; it will keep for up to a week. Enjoy this basbaas with pan-fried fish or kalamuudo (page 165).

Basbaas Qumbe *(COCONUT HOT SAUCE)*

MAKES 2¼ CUPS (530 ML)

1 cup (240 ml) hot water

⅔ cup (54 g) unsweetened shredded coconut

2¾ ounces (80 g) small fresh green Thai chiles (about 40), chopped

¼ small white onion

4 garlic cloves, peeled

Juice of 2 limes

¼ cup (60 ml) distilled white vinegar

2 teaspoons salt

Combine the hot water and shredded coconut in a medium bowl and let sit for 10 minutes.

In a blender, combine the rehydrated coconut along with its soaking water and the chiles, onion, garlic, lime juice, vinegar, and salt; blend until smooth. Serve or refrigerate for later use.

This condiment—the name of which roughly translates to "lick it up"—is mostly eaten in southern Somalia. Semi-ripe mango is sliced and cooked, skin on, with tomato and tamarind paste. The combination of sweetness and tartness from a mango that is not quite ripe pairs very well with the distinct tang of the tamarind and the acidity of the tomatoes. Leeleefow is normally served with afternoon snacks such as sambuus (page 106, 110), nafaqo (page 112), and bajiye (page 116). Sometimes a little basbaas is served as a second condiment alongside the leeleefow. Some people add cornstarch, sweet potatoes, or flour to thicken the leeleefow, but it's not necessary. While mango is relatively low in pectin, the long simmering time allows this sauce to set without any additional thickening agents. Store it in the fridge once it has cooled completely.

Leeleefow *(MANGO-TAMARIND CHUTNEY)*

MAKES ABOUT 1¼ CUPS (300 ML)

1 large green semi-ripe mango, skin on, sliced, and pit retained

1 medium tomato

1½ cups (360 ml) water

1½ ounces (40 g) seedless tamarind paste

½ teaspoon salt

In a medium pot over medium heat, combine the mango pieces (including the pit), tomato, water, tamarind, and salt. Bring to a boil, stir, and cover. Cook, stirring occasionally, for 45 minutes, until the leeleefow has thickened significantly.

Turn the heat down to the lowest setting and cook for another 15 minutes, covered. Remove and discard the mango pit and allow the leeleefow to cool to room temperature before using. Store in the fridge for up to 3 days.

Subag is closer to ghee than to plain clarified butter; the butter is cooked slightly longer for a deeper level of flavor. This recipe uses butter from cow's milk, but subag is often made with goat's milk. Its strong and almost nutty flavor is distinctive—and it can vary depending on the source of the milk. Canjeero (page 80) with subag, oodkac (page 97), and shaah (page 239) is a very traditional Somali breakfast. Subag can also be used in place of butter or oil in desserts, meat dishes, and rice. It's a prized ingredient—one of the most popular foods brought back from Somalia by those in the diaspora. When making it, use unsalted butter as the base so that your subag can be used in a variety of dishes. Always use a clean, dry spoon when doling out the subag to avoid cross contamination and ensure a longer shelf life.

Subag *(GHEE)*

MAKES ABOUT 2 CUPS (450 G)

1 pound (450 g) unsalted butter, at room temperature

In a metal pot, cook the butter over medium heat, uncovered, for about 10 minutes, stirring occasionally. When the butter starts a slow boil and curds begin to form, lower the heat to the lowest setting and cook for 20 more minutes, stirring occasionally, until the curds brown lightly at the bottom.

Take the pot off the stove when the liquid is golden brown and the curds at the bottom are a slightly darker brown but not burnt. Let the subag cool to room temperature, then strain the golden liquid through cheesecloth or a fine-mesh strainer into an airtight container and discard the strained-out solids. Stir for an airier texture and store the subag in the fridge for up to a month.

CHAPTER 4

Morning

Canjeero (pronounced *ahn-je-ro*) is also known as laxoox (*la-hoh*) or anjeelo (*ahn-je-lo*), depending on the region. This sourdough pancake, a cousin of Ethiopian injera and Indian dosas, is one of the most recognizable foods in Somali cuisine. Canjeero batter is typically mixed at night—the distinctive slapping sounds of canjeero batter being beaten is a core childhood memory for many people. After it's mixed, the batter is left to ferment overnight and the pancakes are made the next morning.

This version uses wheat and corn flours, though sorghum is also commonly used in Somalia. In the diaspora, many have found alternative ways to make canjeero, using store-bought pancake mix or alternate flours (like oat flour). These alternatives help make a quicker canjeero that doesn't require as much fermentation. The longer you ferment your batter, the more sour and tangy your canjeero becomes. It's common to save a little bit of the batter to use as a starter for the next batch.

Canjeero is covered while it's cooking; steam contributes to its texture and appearance, and the sizzle sounds of moisture hitting the skillet is an indication that the canjeero may be ready. It's properly made if it has little air bubbles called indho (eyes) and a spiral pattern achieved by adding the batter to the pan in a circular motion from the center to the edges.

Canjeero *(SOURDOUGH PANCAKE)*

MAKES 12 (9½-INCH / 24 CM) PANCAKES

2 teaspoons active dry yeast

2 cups plus 4 teaspoons (500 ml) warm water

2 cups (256 g) all-purpose flour

1 cup plus 2 tablespoons (128 g) white corn flour

Pinch of fine sea salt

Vegetable oil, for greasing the pan

In a large bowl, combine the yeast and ¼ cup (60 ml) of the warm water; wait 10 minutes for the yeast to activate. When the yeast is foamy, add the all-purpose flour, corn flour, salt, and 1¼ cups (300 ml) of the warm water and mix with your hand until evenly incorporated. Then, using a downward scooping motion, pick the thick batter up and slap it into the bowl using your palm for 5 minutes.

Add the remaining ½ cup plus 4 teaspoons (140 ml) water and mix it into the dough. Cover the bowl with a lid or plastic wrap and set aside at room temperature to allow the dough to rise overnight.

The next day, mix the separated batter back into itself until it's smooth and slightly thinner than pancake batter. Grease a 10-inch (25 cm) nonstick crepe pan or cast-iron griddle with oil (spread it with a paper towel) and heat the pan over medium-high heat until it's hot but not smoking. Ladle ¼ cup (60 ml) of the batter into the center of the hot pan and spread it in a circular swirling motion, starting from the center and working outward to the edges, as far as the batter will allow. The canjeero batter should look like a spiral. Immediately cover the pan with a lid and cook until the canjeero is brown on the bottom and the batter has dried, 1 to 2 minutes.

Remove the lid and transfer the canjeero from the pan to a plate; cover with a second plate so the pancake doesn't dry out. Repeat the process until all the batter has been used, greasing the pan as needed so the canjeero doesn't stick. Serve warm.

ON FUSION, FORCED MIGRATION, AND SOMALI FOOD

In 2021, I launched a pop-up in Los Angeles that featured a culinary idea I had been toying with for over a decade. In a city that famously loves breakfast burritos, I began to sell a Somali-style wrap—spongy and sour canjeero-wrapped breakfast burritos filled with soft scrambled eggs, fuul (fava bean stew), and spicy, vibrant green basbaas (Somali hot sauce). To my surprise and delight, I sold out week after week—despite the fact that, for many of my LA customers, this was their first introduction to Somali cuisine.

I grew up eating fuul, eggs, and canjeero. For me, the burrito was a way to share a favorite family breakfast—the only difference was that my version rolled the ingredients straight into the soft sourdough canjeero with its bubble-lined pockets.

In this, as in my other pop-ups, I enjoyed reinterpreting classic Somali cuisine with care and intention. Occasionally, though, fellow members of the Somali diaspora have labeled what I do as "fusion" cuisine.

I don't think of my food as fusion food; rather, it is classic Somali cuisine *reimagined*. This reimagining is rooted in my knowing and respecting the classic form of the cuisine, then building on it. It is fluid—it adheres to classicism and flirts with creativity. It rests on the cuisine's ability to expand depending on what new shores it meets through migration—in our case, a forced migration.

The famous Somali poet Warsan Shire writes: "No one leaves home unless / home is the mouth of a shark / you only run for the border / when you see the whole city running as well." When the Somali Civil War broke out in 1991, my family and I became refugees. We spent the next several years in search of safety and home, first in neighboring East African countries and finally, permanently, settling in a rainy city called Seattle. My family remains there, but we are not fully assimilated—it's as if we've anticipated that our lives in the US will only be temporary.

The thing about having endured a forced migration is that, mentally, your bags are always packed. Even if you've lived somewhere for nearly thirty years, you feel like you could go home—to your real home—any day. You remain in a decades-long emotional limbo. This feeling is not unique to me and my family; it's something you can see on the faces and sense in the spirits of all people who leave home by force. Forced migration is not only an absence of choice; it ruptures whole communities, resulting in the absence of "home."

Many Somalis in the diaspora must balance that experience of rupture and absence with the influences of the culture of wherever we're living. Forced into migration, we are acutely (and chronically) disoriented, simultaneously living between and outside each culture.

In this context, it's complicated for me to navigate others' policing of the Somali-ness of my cooking. In the last few years, food writers have increased the critical focus on fusion cuisine. Writer Soleil Ho differentiates "fusion food" from "assimilation food"; others have referred to "in-between food." But no matter what people choose to call diaspora cooking, its authenticity is perpetually in question. Some label my cooking as fusion solely because of my location. But at what point do diaspora foods become an accepted part of a culinary tradition, seeded and sprouted into the cuisine of a nation or a people? Considering the inevitable evolution of all cuisines, who within a community has authority as a gatekeeper and judge of authenticity?

As a chef, I've wondered whether the fusion label ever applies to cooking done in one's homeland. Is food deemed authentic only when experimentation happens in the "right" geographical location? I'm constantly examining what terms like "classic," "traditional," or "authentic" mean. On a homecoming trip in 2018, I arrived in Mogadishu having internalized the idea that the most correct Somali cuisine awaited me in Somalia—that the global Somali diaspora could only offer a sliver of the real thing.

In Mogadishu, I encountered a food culture that was alive and constantly shifting. This vibrancy was particularly evident in the experimental street foods I had the luck of eating, such as leeleefow—a mixed mango-tamarind chutney—served atop fried foods like sambuus or bajiye. I found myself astonished by Somalis' enthusiasm for foods from abroad, such as Mexican tres leches cake and Thai ice cream roll-ups. It wasn't that I consciously thought that this level of experimentation and adoption couldn't occur. It was that, as a member of the diaspora, I had implicitly been taught that in Somalia, the culinary environment would be entirely devoted to the most classic forms of Somali cuisine.

But my time in Mogadishu helped me realize that we in the diaspora may actually be the most attached to the concept of "classic" Somali cuisine. Like many other immigrants and refugees, our cultural consciousness was frozen in the time that we or our parents left our homelands. I read once that many Somali living rooms in the diaspora prioritize 1980s-style curtain décor, reflecting the last time many of our families knew peace before the Civil War. In a way, this mindset is reflected in every other aspect of Somali diasporic existence. That time before the war became a memorialized safe space, a nostalgic mental refuge to return to again and again.

Our culinary memory is no exception. Our dishes and traditions have remained unchanged by time as we dedicated ourselves to preserving the classical and "purest" forms of Somali culture and cuisine—the last things we had known at home, and at peace. Forced migration meant we clung to what was most familiar, while trauma made us need to protect and maintain what we once knew, just as we knew it.

Our brothers and sisters in Somalia who never left did not have the same experiences or conditions. Those who stayed through the war and who were born into or after the war were freer to experiment within their culture. Somali cuisine in Somalia was allowed to shift and expand and bloom, as any cuisine inevitably does. There was nothing to prove—no loss of identity to fear. They were already home.

It's no wonder, then, that it's the diaspora that clings so desperately to "classic" cuisine. It's a bridge connecting us back to the homeland—understandable, but also a crutch (and, of course, migration and location impact what foods are available to us). Culinary traditions shape-shift depending on community—whether it's the Somali diaspora in Minneapolis, Minnesota, or the Somali diaspora in Melbourne, Australia. It's a tale as old as time—immigrants and refugees learn to adapt to their new environments and make do with what they have access to.

I've seen the beginnings of a new generation of Somalis in the diaspora who are breaking away from the "classic" mold and seem to feel less pressure to prove the authenticity of their Somali-ness. This may be due to generational distance from the trauma of forced migration and from nostalgia for a prewar life, or maybe it just reflects their lived experiences.

These are people like my colleague and fellow millennial Somali chef Jamal Hashi (see page 148), who created a camel-meat hamburger that introduced a new way for people to enjoy a Somali culinary mainstay. Or they may be second-generation Gen Z–aged diaspora kids on TikTok sharing videos of dishes like shaah (Somali tea) ice cream—dishes that reflect *all* their cultural influences. What is clear is that there are millions of ways to belong to a diaspora and to live authentically within a culture.

Are my canjeero burritos fusion food if I haven't changed the original ingredients? I don't believe so. Are they a classic Somali food widely known to everyone, everywhere in the diaspora? Definitely not. Are they a traditional food? Maybe just to my family! But I do know one thing for sure: They are authentic to me.

Sorghum has been grown in Somalia for centuries and is a vital part of the indigenous cuisine. While there has been a shift away from this healthy grain, it still remains as an important part of the ancestral Somali diet. This warming porridge has long been eaten by agricultural workers cultivating the land. It is made from soaked whole grains that are then ground using a traditional grinding method. It is not uncommon for people to mix different types of grains to make their own porridge blend. This porridge is made with sorghum flour and is on the thinner side; for a thicker porridge, reduce the amount of water by a cup or so. Mixing the sorghum flour with cold water first keeps the batter from clumping. Instead of sugar, you can use another sweetener like honey or maple syrup.

Mishaari Masaggo *(SORGHUM PORRIDGE)*

SERVES 2 TO 3

3 cups (720 ml) water

1 cup (128 g) sorghum flour

2 cups (480 ml) milk

¼ teaspoon fine sea salt

¼ cup (50 g) sugar, or to taste

Buttermilk or milk, for serving

Ghee, butter, or sesame oil, for serving

In a small bowl, mix 1 cup of the water and the sorghum flour together until there are no clumps. Set aside.

Place a medium pot over medium heat. Add the milk, salt, and remaining 2 cups of water to the pot. Whisk in the sorghum and water mixture until it's fully incorporated.

Stir continuously until the porridge thickens, about 5 minutes. Mix in the sugar, cover, and let the porridge cook over medium-low heat for 15 minutes, stirring and adjusting the heat as needed so as to avoid burning or overflow. Serve hot with milk or buttermilk and top with ghee, butter, or sesame oil as you like.

Boorash has a smooth texture and is a comforting alternative to chunkier oatmeal. It is not only a breakfast staple but something served to the sick and to new mothers, and as a baby's first food. While oats are now commonly used in the porridge that is served to new mothers, traditionally sorghum would have been used. Ground nigella seed, which has healing properties according to Islamic medicine, may also be added, as may black pepper, for a slight hint of spice. Feel free to add a little subag (ghee) to the finished porridge for a richer, nuttier flavor.

Boorash *(OAT PORRIDGE)*

SERVES 4

2⅓ cups (190 g) rolled oats

4 cups (960 ml) water

2 cups (480 ml) milk, plus more to serve

¼ teaspoon fine sea salt

¼ teaspoon ground black pepper (optional)

¼ cup (50 g) sugar or other sweetener of choice (to taste)

Combine the oats, water, milk, salt, pepper (if using), and sugar in a blender and blend until smooth. Transfer the mixture to a medium pot, set over medium heat, and stir until the porridge thickens, 4 to 5 minutes. Turn the heat down to low, cover the pot, and cook the oats for 25 minutes, stirring occasionally. Add water as needed if the porridge is too thick for your liking. Serve warm, with additional milk if you like.

Qado (lunch) is the most important meal of the day, so people don't normally eat a heavy quraac (breakfast). It is not uncommon just to have shaah (tea) or qaxwo (coffee) with a few pieces of canjeero; some kind of protein with canjeero; or a porridge such as mishaari masaggo or boorash. The morning is a busy time for many families, so light, easy foods are preferred. In Somalia, canjeero batter is mixed in most households at night in order to serve it to the family for breakfast the next day. In the diaspora, people often eat their own individual meals, and since canjeero is sometimes seen as time-consuming, it is often saved for the weekends when there is more time and families are at home together.

Malawax (pronounced *ma-la-wah*) is a thin, fragrant crepe usually made with cardamom and eaten for breakfast or as a snack. It is also one of my favorite Somali foods. Originally, it was made from water and flour only, but over time it has evolved to include eggs, milk, cardamom, and sometimes, cinnamon. Unlike canjeero, malawax is cooked on both sides, allowing little golden-brown pockets to form all over the surface. It's moist and light and distinctly sweeter than canjeero thanks to the drizzle of ghee and dusting of sugar on it, and it also has delicious crispy edges. Do make sure to spread a little ghee in the pan with a paper towel between each malawax so they don't stick. These are made to share and are best enjoyed warm with a cup of coffee or tea.

Malawax *(CARDAMOM CREPE)*

MAKES 8 TO 10 MALAWAX

- 1⅓ cups (170 g) all-purpose flour
- 1 cup (240 ml) milk
- 1 cup (240 ml) water
- 1 large egg
- ¼ cup (50 g) sugar, plus more for serving
- 1 teaspoon ground cardamom
- ¼ teaspoon cinnamon (optional)
- Melted ghee, as needed

In a blender, combine the flour, milk, water, egg, sugar, cardamom, and cinnamon (if using) and blend until smooth. Transfer to a large bowl.

Lightly grease a nonstick crepe pan or griddle with ghee. Set the pan over medium-high heat until hot but not smoking, then ladle ⅓ cup of the batter into the pan, spreading it in light swirls to ensure its thickness is completely even.

Cook until the bottom is light brown and the batter is no longer liquid, 1 to 2 minutes. Drizzle the top of the malawax with ½ teaspoon of melted ghee, then flip it. Cook for 20 seconds or so, until little brown pockets form all over the surface. Using a spatula, flip the malawax onto a plate and dust it with however much sugar you'd like. Repeat the process until the batter is gone and you have a stack; serve while still warm.

This dish is a childhood favorite of mine, and it was in frequent rotation during my traditional forty-day postpartum period at home. For many in the diaspora, it's a favorite because of the way it stretches to feed an entire household cheaply using basic pantry ingredients. This scramble comes together quickly: It's a deeply comforting dish with a mild flavor—and a great source of protein. If you like, serve it with canjeero or crusty French bread and a hot cup of shaah.

Ukun iyo Mallaay *(EGG AND TUNA SCRAMBLE)*

SERVES 2 TO 3

1 tablespoon oil

½ red onion, halved and sliced

1 (5-ounce / 142 g) can yellowfin tuna in olive oil

6 large eggs, beaten

¾ teaspoon salt, or to taste

In a skillet, heat the oil over medium-high heat. When the oil is shimmering, after about 1 minute, add the onion. Cook, stirring occasionally, until the onion softens, 5 to 6 minutes.

Stir in the tuna with its oil and cover the pan; cook over medium heat for 5 minutes. Meanwhile, beat the eggs and salt together in a medium bowl. Uncover the pan and pour in the beaten eggs.

Don't stir the eggs; cover the pan and let them settle into the tuna for 15 or 20 seconds. Uncover the pan and gently stir for about 2 minutes, until a cohesive egg and tuna scramble forms. Transfer to plates and serve immediately.

In this Somali version of shakshuka, the eggs are scrambled and cooked with bell peppers, tomatoes, onions, cilantro, and spicy peppers. Despite the jalapeño, this dish is not overwhelmingly hot—it simply has a nice bite of heat. Make sure to cover the shakshuuko during the cooking process to keep the eggs from drying out. This dish is best enjoyed right away, either on its own or with canjeero or another bread of your choice.

Shakshuuko *(EGG AND TOMATO SCRAMBLE)*

SERVES 2 OR 3

2 tablespoons olive oil

1 small red onion, halved and sliced

1 small-to-medium jalapeño pepper, halved

½ small green bell pepper, sliced

3 medium tomatoes, chopped

2 garlic cloves, smashed or minced

⅓ cup (5 g) coarsely chopped cilantro leaves

4 large eggs

1 teaspoon fine sea salt

Ground black pepper to taste

Canjeero, for serving (optional)

In a large skillet, heat the oil over medium-high heat until shimmering. Add the onion and jalapeño and cook, uncovered, for 5 minutes, stirring occasionally, until the onion and jalapeño have softened slightly.

Add the bell pepper, tomatoes, garlic, and cilantro; stir and cover. Cook, stirring occasionally, until the tomatoes have broken down completely, about 10 to 15 minutes. If more oil is needed to keep things from sticking, add a splash.

Beat the eggs and salt together in a medium bowl and add them to the tomatoes; do not stir. Allow the eggs to settle into the pan and begin to cook, 15 to 20 seconds, then mix gently to fully incorporate the eggs into the vegetables. While the eggs are still semi-runny, cover the pan for 1 minute and lower the heat to medium. Uncover and gently fold the eggs together, then take the skillet off the burner and serve the scramble immediately, on its own or with canjeero.

BARLIN ALI, COOKBOOK AUTHOR

Long before Barlin Ali wrote the first mainstream Somali cookbook, she was a teenager in Somalia with zero cooking skills. A recently married Barlin, tasked with making dinner for visiting relatives, made a dinner so disastrous that her brother-in-law took her to Shabelle, a popular Italian restaurant in Mogadishu, and asked the Somali chef, Hassan, to give her paid cooking lessons. Hassan agreed, and his weekly lessons set Barlin on an unexpected path.

Born in the late 1950s, Barlin grew up splitting her time between Mogadishu and her grandmother's farm in Buur Hakaba, three hours northwest of the city. The Mogadishu of Barlin's childhood was a cosmopolitan city whose food reflected the many cultural influences there, with Somali, Italian, and Arab dishes. She has fond memories of men in her neighborhood going door to door with freshly caught fish, of enjoying handmade pasta at outdoor restaurants in the city, and of eating freshly grown vegetables on visits to her grandmother. While most Somali girls begin their culinary education early, Barlin was often shooed out of the kitchen by her mother and sister, who were both wonderful cooks. She recalls her mother making flavorful rice and meat dishes over coals in a traditional Somali cooking utensil called a burjiiko.

In young adulthood, as her cooking lessons continued, Barlin began experimenting in the kitchen. In the early 1980s, she also began traveling outside of Somalia, attending school in Michigan in 1982 and visiting New York in 1984. She was on vacation in the US in 1988 when the rumblings of an imminent war began in Somalia, and she was advised not to return. She settled in Virginia and spent the next several decades there with her family, working for USAID as a senior diaspora advisor.

When Barlin and her family first arrived in the Washington, DC, area in 1988, there were very few Somalis living there—just a handful of professionals who would gather on weekends to break bread and to enjoy each other's company. It was during this time in Virginia that Barlin really began to build her reputation as a cook. She brought sambuus to work or school potlucks, and people would ask her for her recipes. She also began catering, and her food was such a hit that colleagues and acquaintances would ask if there was a Somali cookbook they could purchase.

Other than Asha Mohamud Guled's 1978 book, which Barlin found at the Library of Congress, there were no Somali cookbooks in existence. Wanting to remedy the fundamental lack of understanding around Somali food culture and cuisine and meet the cultural hunger of Somali kids born in the US, she began working on a Somali cookbook.

Barlin's pioneering book, *Somali Cuisine*, would take her four years to complete, with assistance from her mother and her sister (who had opened a restaurant called Nel Continente Nero in Genoa, Italy). She did not have a literary agent and spent those years shopping her book around to publishers as well as carefully writing and testing

recipes. She had her work cut out for her: Somali cuisine is an oral tradition, passed down without written measurements.

Somali Cuisine was published in 2007, opening up the Somali cookbook space. With recipes ranging from appetizers and mains to desserts and drinks, as well as stories from Barlin's childhood in Somalia, the book was well received. She toured the country, sharing the book in Somali diaspora hubs across America and giving a talk at the Library of Congress (which also houses a copy of the book).

However, with success inevitably comes criticism. Some in the community didn't understand why she had "wasted her time" writing a Somali cookbook: Somalis already know how to make Somali food! These naysayers didn't understand either the cultural and culinary preservation work Barlin had undertaken or the ways the war—and the diaspora—had impacted Somali foodways.

Others, with limited knowledge of regional cooking, went so far as to dispute the existence of recipes in her book—some of which she herself had grown up eating. One such was deggo, a minced beef and tomato sauce often served in the 1970s at a popular restaurant called Hassan's, in Mogadishu's Shangani neighborhood.

Some recipes that Barlin grew up eating, and that have largely disappeared from the minds of Somalis, were not in the book, like bariis talyaani, a milky, sweetly spiced rice pudding made during Ramadan, and an obvious relic of the time of Italian colonialism.

Over the phone with me, Barlin speaks with deep knowledge about disappearing Somali culinary traditions and cooking practices, such as the method of cooking with traditional Somali clayware called dheri. She also speaks of the collapse of knowledge of regionally specific cuisines and the ways the war and the diaspora it created made for narrower, fixed ideas of what Somali cuisine is—so much so that, for example, when particular ingredients are used in a dish, those who did not grow up using them question their existence in Somali cuisine.

One such example is nutmeg, which Barlin saw being added to savory dishes like risotto or used as the defining ingredient in a dessert called xalwo hilaal. She also acknowledges the evolution of dishes, particularly nationally loved, universal dishes like canjeero, which went from using corn and sorghum flours to incorporating other grains and even seeds.

After her cookbook was published, Barlin started a tea business. It flourished, and she began providing Somali tea to restaurants in the DC area. In 2015, she began teaching Somali cooking classes that were so popular they had a waiting list. She continued catering events for institutions like the World Bank and the Library of Congress, including one event celebrating the fiftieth anniversary of Peace Corps volunteers in Somalia.

In 2018, Barlin shut down her tea business, retired from her USAID job, and quietly relocated to Hargeisa. Today she lives with her husband on a beautiful homestead, growing her own fruits and vegetables, making her own jam and cheese, and visiting the local market, where she continues to marvel at the ways Somali food keeps expanding and shifting over time. Barlin's dedicated preservation of Somali foodways means that generations of Somalis in the global diaspora can connect with their culinary heritage and share it with each other and the world. (It also goes without saying that her cookbook *Somali Cuisine* is a foundational text in Somali cookery—and it paved the way for the existence of this cookbook!)

Killi is considered a delicacy; it's also part of a traditional Somali breakfast. It can be made from goat, lamb, or cow kidney. While its ingredients are very simple, it's loved for its deep, rich flavor—though for some, kidney may be an acquired taste. It's important to remove the white fatty tissue before cooking; if you go to a Somali butcher, they can remove it and cut the meat for you. The sautéed peppers and onions really bring this dish to life. Serve killi with canjeero or malawax for a sweet and savory contrast of flavors.

Killi *(KIDNEY, PEPPERS, AND ONIONS)*

SERVES 2 OR 3

3 tablespoons olive oil

½ red onion, halved and sliced

1 pound (450 g) goat kidney, white tissue removed, cut into bite-sized pieces

1 teaspoon salt

½ medium green bell pepper, sliced

Canjeero (page 80), Malawax (page 89), or bread of your choice, for serving

In a medium skillet over medium-high heat, heat the oil for 1 minute, or until shimmering. Add half of the onion and cook, stirring occasionally, for 6 minutes, or until the onions have softened.

Add the kidney, sprinkle over the salt, and cook for 10 minutes, stirring continuously until any liquid the kidney has produced is almost gone.

Add the remaining onion and the sliced pepper and cook for 5 minutes over medium heat, until the peppers and onion are tender but not mushy. Remove the killi from the stove and serve immediately with canjeero, malawax, or a bread of your choosing.

This preserved beef, known as both oodkac and muqmad, is part of Somalia's nomadic heritage. Traditionally, it's made by drying strips of camel meat in the sun, then, later, frying the meat in ghee with salt. Drying allowed Somalis to eat meat while on long journeys. This dish is also eaten at times of celebration. In the north, there is a wedding tradition called xeedho (or xeero), wherein a container holding the oodkac is topped and sealed with mashed dates and ghee. It is then placed in a larger container that is decorated with leather, cloth, and small shells and sealed by the family of the bride, who present it to the groom's family. They have to open the container, which is meant to represent the bride: If they are unable to do so, the bride's family can take her back.

In the diaspora, oodkac is typically made from beef, which is more widely available than camel. Goat or lamb meat can also be used. If you can't find the meat in a Somali store, ask a butcher to cut the beef into ¼ inch cubes. These days, it's a popular breakfast, eaten in the morning with canjeero soaked in ghee and tea with sugar. The salty, nutty flavor of the oodkac balances beautifully with the sweetness of the tea and the sour, buttery canjeero. Oodkac keeps for up to a week in an airtight container in the fridge. Always spoon some out with a dry, clean spoon to delay spoilage.

Oodkac *(BEEF JERKY)*

SERVES 6 TO 8

2½ pounds (1.1 kg) beef stew meat, cut into ¼-inch cubes

1½ teaspoons salt

Seeds from 10 green cardamom pods, crushed (shells discarded)

2 cups (480 ml) vegetable oil

1 cup (240 ml) ghee

In a medium pot over medium-high heat, cook the beef uncovered for 15 minutes, stirring often and breaking up clumps as it cooks until it is no longer red.

Add the salt and cardamom and, stirring continuously, turn the heat up to high to evaporate all the liquid the beef has produced, about 10 minutes. Add the oil and ghee as soon as the liquid is gone, and turn the heat down to medium-high. Bring the oil to a boil and, stirring constantly so nothing burns, cook the meat until it is browned, about 10 minutes. Take the pot off the heat and let everything cool to room temperature. The meat will continue to cook in the oil as it cools; when it's done it should be dark brown in color. Store the meat in its cooking fat in an airtight container in the fridge for up to a week.

Sareen is comforting, filling, and healthy and can keep one satiated throughout the day; this makes it a popular choice during Ramadan for suhoor (the meal before sunrise). Its toppings are many and include milk, subag (ghee), and sesame oil; this recipe uses buttermilk and sugar to make it a sweet and tangy meal. The barley requires a lot of water and time; the longer you cook it, the more tender it will become. Serve sareen for breakfast or as a light supper; it can be made into a savory dish by omitting the sweetener and buttermilk and cooking the sareen as you would rice, with your choice of added meat and vegetables.

Sareen iyo Garoor *(PEARL BARLEY AND BUTTERMILK)*

SERVES 4

8 cups (1.9 L) water

½ teaspoon fine sea salt

1 cup (200 g) pearl barley

Buttermilk, for serving

Sugar, honey, or maple syrup, for serving

In a large pot, combine 7 cups of the water with the salt and bring to a boil over high heat.

Add the barley, lower the heat to medium-high, and cook, uncovered, for 1 hour, stirring occasionally.

After the first hour, add the final cup of water, cover and reduce the heat to low, and cook for another hour. Take the pot off the heat and serve hot topped with buttermilk and sugar or the sweetener of your choice.

Cambaabur is a sourdough pancake eaten in Borama and Hargeisa, as well as Djibouti (formerly French Somaliland), a Somali-majority nation. It is very similar to canjeero, but it has a deep golden color (from the addition of turmeric) and is flavored by fennel and nigella seeds, as well as garlic and onion. Cambaabur is typically eaten on the morning of Eid. Traditionally, it was served on its own with ghee or honey; now it's often topped with plain yogurt and sugar or with thick buttermilk.

Cambaabur *(SPICED SOURDOUGH PANCAKES)*

MAKES 12 (9½-INCH / 24 CM) PANCAKES

- 2½ cups (600 ml) warm water, divided
- ¾ tablespoon active dry yeast
- ¼ small white onion, sliced
- 1 garlic clove
- 1½ teaspoons ground turmeric
- ½ teaspoon fennel seeds
- ½ teaspoon nigella seeds
- 2 cups (256 g) all-purpose flour
- 1 cup (130 g) sorghum flour
- Pinch of fine sea salt
- Canola oil or ghee, for greasing
- Plain yogurt or buttermilk, for serving
- Sugar, for serving
- Ghee, for serving

In a large bowl, combine ¼ cup (60 ml) of the water and yeast and set aside for 10 minutes for the yeast to activate.

In a blender, combine ¼ cup (60 ml) of the water with the onion, garlic, turmeric, fennel seeds, and nigella seeds and blend until smooth; set aside.

When the yeast is foamy, add the all-purpose flour, sorghum flour, salt, and 1 cup (240 ml) of water and mix with your hand until evenly incorporated. Then, using a downward scooping motion, pick the thick batter up and slap it into the bowl using your palm for 5 minutes—the dough will be sticky. Add the remaining 1 cup (240 ml) water and the blended onion mixture to the batter; stir to combine. Cover the bowl with plastic wrap and set aside at room temperature to allow the dough to rise overnight.

The next day, whisk the separated batter back into itself until it's smooth and thinner than pancake batter. Grease a nonstick crepe pan with oil and heat the pan over medium-high heat until it's hot but not smoking. Ladle ⅓ cup (80 ml) of batter into the center of the hot pan and spread it in a circular swirling motion, starting from the center and working outward to the edges, as far as the batter will allow. Immediately cover the pan with a lid and cook until the cambaabur is brown on the bottom and the batter has dried, 1 to 2 minutes.

Transfer the cambaabur to a plate; cover with a second plate so the pancake doesn't dry out. Repeat the process until all the batter has been used, greasing the pan as necessary. Serve with yogurt or buttermilk, sugar, and ghee.

This umami-packed dish is a favorite breakfast in many Somali households: It's simple, comes together quickly, and is high in both flavor and nutrients (especially iron). Unlike killi (kidney), beer (liver) does not produce extra liquid when it's cooking, so you'll need to add in a little water. Enjoy this dish in the morning with canjeero or some crusty French bread to soak up all the flavors.

Beer *(LIVER AND ONIONS)*

SERVES 2 OR 3

3 tablespoons olive oil

½ red onion, halved and sliced

1 pound (450 g) lamb liver, sliced into strips

1 teaspoon salt

½ medium green bell pepper, sliced

¼ cup (60 ml) water

Canjeero (page 80) or other bread of choice, for serving

Place a medium skillet over medium-high heat and add the oil. Once it's shimmering, add half of the onion and cook for 1 minute. Add the liver, sprinkle with the salt, and stir continuously for 4 minutes, then add the remaining onion and the bell pepper and cook for 4 more minutes, until the liver is browned and the peppers and onions have softened slightly. Add the water and cook for 1 minute, then take the pan off the stove. Serve immediately with canjeero.

CHAPTER 5

Casariyo *(AFTERNOON TEA)*

Sambuus is a cousin of the Indian samosa. While some people do use *sambuus* and *samosa* interchangeably (particularly in countries along the Swahili coast), they have quite a few differences. Hilib (beef) is by far the most well-known sambuus filling, and this sambuus gets its distinctly Somali flavor from the spice mix xawaash. Sambuus is most often made during Ramadan and served as a delicious treat after a long day of fasting, often paired with a sweet pastry like bur (page 119). Note that this recipe makes 16 wrappers but the filling works for 11 sambuus. The wrappers, filling, and the folded sambuus all freeze well.

Sambuus Hilib *(FRIED BEEF DUMPLINGS)*

MAKES 11 SAMBUUS

For the Wrappers

3 cups (384 g) all-purpose flour, plus for more dusting

A scant 1 cup (230 ml) water

¼ cup (60 ml) canola oil, plus more for oiling dough and greasing hands

½ teaspoon salt

For the Paste

1 cup (128 g) all-purpose flour

1 cup (240 ml) water

For the Filling

1 pound (450 g) ground beef

1 large red onion, minced finely

⅔ cup (10 g) finely chopped cilantro leaves and tender stems

5 garlic cloves, smashed or minced

1½ tablespoons olive oil

1 tablespoon Xawaash (page 56)

1½ teaspoons salt

To Finish

Vegetable or canola oil, for frying

Basbaas (page 63), for serving

To make the wrapper dough, combine the flour, water, oil, and salt in a large bowl. Stir, then knead for about 6 minutes in the bowl, until a smooth dough comes together. Cover with a tea towel and set aside in a warm place to rest for 45 minutes.

Generously oil a work surface and lightly dust with flour. Separate the dough into four equal balls, then roll each ball into a rough 15-inch (38 cm) circle. With a brush or paper towel, lightly oil the top of each circle of dough and then dust with flour. Stack two pieces of dough and trim the edges with a knife to make a perfect 13-inch (33 cm) circle (use a 13-inch / 33 cm circle of waxed paper as a template if you like). Cut the round into four quarters. Repeat with the other two pieces of rolled-out dough. In total, there should be 8 two-layer dough pieces of equal size.

Heat a large nonstick pan over medium-low heat. Add one stacked piece of dough to the pan and toast it for 1 minute, until light-brown specks appear on its underside; flip and toast the second side for 30 seconds. Remove the dough from the pan and set it on a plate to cool. Repeat the process with the remaining 7 dough pieces. When each toasted dough piece is cool, pull the two pieces apart so that you have 16 sambuus wrappers; set these aside while you make the paste and the filling.

To make the paste, stir together the flour and water in a small bowl to form a thick paste. Set aside.

To make the filling, heat a medium skillet over medium-high heat, add the ground beef, and brown, stirring and breaking chunks apart as it cooks, about 3 minutes. Add the onion, cilantro, garlic, oil, xawaash, and salt to the pan and cook for another 10 minutes over medium low heat, stirring occasionally. Take the pan off the heat and let the filling cool completely.

When you're ready to assemble the sambuus, line a large plate with parchment and set it beside a clean work surface. Dust the surface generously with flour. Place one sambuus wrapper on the surface with the rounded side toward you. Lift the bottom left corner and fold it over halfway to the middle of the quarter circle. Dip two fingers into the flour paste and swipe it all over the folded section. Grasp the right corner of the quarter-circle and fold it over the section with the paste to evenly cover it; press down. You should now have a cone.

Lift the cone and cradle it in one hand with the opening facing up; fill the cone two-thirds of the way with a small spoonful of filling and tuck the tips from the overlapping sides over the top of the filling. Next, using your fingers, spread paste onto the center flap of the sambuus cone, then press it down so that the filling is sealed into a triangular sambuus. Set the sambuus down on the parchment-lined plate and repeat the process until all the filling is gone. If any have holes, pinch gently together, using any extra paste as glue. Any remaining wrappers will freeze well.

To cook the sambuus, pour canola oil into a deep skillet or pot about ½ inch (1.3 cm) deep and set over medium-high heat. Place a paper towel–lined plate or colander beside the skillet. Once the oil is shimmering, add two to three sambuus, spacing them out so they don't touch. Fry for 1 to 2 minutes on one side, then turn with tongs and fry another 30 seconds, until the sambuus are golden brown and crispy all over. With the tongs, transfer the sambuus from the oil to the paper towel–lined plate. Repeat until all the sambuus have been fried. Serve hot with basbaas on the side.

CASARIYO (AFTERNOON TEA)

Somalia has a vibrant afternoon tea culture. This midday meal, typically served after lunch and before casho (dinner)—after the asr Islamic prayer—is called casariyo (pronounced *ah-sa-riyo*). It's a time for people to rest and nourish themselves, whether on their own or in a group. Families, friends, and neighbors come together to eat sweet and savory foods like sambuus, bur, and bajiye and to drink coffee or tea. Some casariyo foods are made at home, and some are street foods. The point is that casariyo is an opportunity to slow down, rest, and catch up with others in the middle of the day. (Café gatherings, which have a similar cultural role, are also big amongst Somalis—particularly the men—both in Somalia and in the diaspora.) While daily casariyo is harder to observe in the diaspora, many Somalis have maintained the tradition—even if only on the weekend.

While hilib (beef) may be the most well-known sambuus filling, tuna is not far behind. There are also coconut sambuus (popular in Somalia), chicken sambuus, vegetable sambuus, camel sambuus, and salmon sambuus (popular among Somali Americans in the Pacific Northwest). But tuuna sambuus is a staple throughout the diaspora, where canned tuna is a readily available and familiar staple. Sambuus wrappers are typically made with all-purpose flour, but sorghum flour is traditional as well. This recipe allows you to make sambuus wrappers by hand, but Somalis in the diaspora use what is accessible to wrap sambuus, from tortillas to egg roll wraps. This recipe makes 11 sambuus, and any leftover sambuus wrappers can be frozen for later use. The recipe can also be doubled to feed a crowd.

Sambuus Tuuna *(FRIED TUNA DUMPLINGS)*

MAKES 11 SAMBUUS

For the Wrappers

3 cups (384 g) all-purpose flour, plus for more dusting

A scant 1 cup (230 ml) water

¼ cup (60 ml) canola oil, plus more as needed

½ teaspoon salt

For the Paste

1 cup (128 g) all-purpose flour

1 cup (240 ml) water

For the Filling

2 tablespoons canola oil

1 medium red onion, finely diced

8 garlic cloves, smashed

2 teaspoons Xawaash (page 56)

3 (5-ounce / 142 g) cans yellowfin tuna in oil

1 bunch green onions, minced

⅔ cup (10 g) cilantro leaves and tender stems, finely chopped

2½ teaspoons Vegeta seasoning (see page 48)

To Finish

Vegetable or canola oil, for frying

Basbaas (page 63), for serving

To make the wrapper dough, combine the flour, water, oil, and salt in a large bowl. Stir, then knead for about 6 minutes in the bowl, until a smooth dough comes together. Cover with a tea towel and set aside in a warm place to rest for 45 minutes.

Generously dust a work surface with flour. Separate the dough into four equal balls, then roll each ball into a rough 15-inch (38 cm) circle. With a brush or paper towel, lightly oil the top of each circle of dough and then dust with flour. Stack two pieces of dough and trim the edges with a knife to make a perfect 13-inch (33 cm) circle (use a 13-inch / 33 cm circle of waxed paper as a template if you like). Cut the round into four quarters. Repeat with the other two pieces of rolled-out dough. In total, there should be 8 two-layer dough pieces of equal size.

Heat a large nonstick pan over medium-low heat. Add one stacked piece of dough to the pan and toast it for 1 minute, until light-brown specks appear on its underside; flip and toast the second side for 30 seconds. Remove the dough from the pan and set it on a plate to cool. Repeat the process with the remaining 7 dough pieces. When each toasted dough piece is cool, pull the two pieces apart so that you have 16 sambuus wrappers; set these aside while you make the paste and the filling.

To make the paste, stir together the flour and water in a small bowl to form a thick paste. Set aside.

To make the filling, heat the oil in a medium skillet over medium-high heat until it shimmers, about 1 minute. Add the onion and cook, stirring until soft, about 3 minutes. Add the garlic and xawaash and cook until the garlic has crisped slightly, another 30 seconds. Add the tuna with its oil and the green onions, cilantro, and Vegeta seasoning and cook until the tuna has softened and the green onion has wilted slightly, about 5 minutes. Remove the filling from the heat and allow it to cool completely.

When you're ready to assemble the sambuus, line a large plate with parchment and set it beside a clean work surface. Dust the surface generously with flour. Place one sambuus wrapper on the surface with the rounded side toward you. Lift the bottom left corner and fold it over halfway to the middle of the quarter circle. Dip two fingers into the flour paste and swipe it all over the folded section. Grasp the right corner of the quarter-circle and fold it over the section with the paste to evenly cover it; press down. You should now have a cone.

Lift the cone and cradle it in one hand with the opening facing up; fill the cone two-thirds of the way with a small spoonful of filling and tuck the tips from the overlapping sides over the top of the filling. Next, using your fingers, spread paste onto the center flap of the sambuus cone, then press it down so that the filling is sealed into a triangular sambuus. Set the sambuus down on the parchment-lined plate and repeat the process until all the filling is gone. If any have holes, pinch gently together, using any extra paste as glue. Any remaining wrappers will freeze well.

To cook the sambuus, pour canola oil into a deep skillet or pot about ½ inch (1.3 cm) deep and set over medium-high heat. Place a paper towel–lined plate or colander beside the skillet. Once the oil is shimmering, add two to three sambuus, spacing them out so they don't touch. Fry for 1 to 2 minutes on one side, then turn with tongs and fry another 30 seconds, until the sambuus are golden brown and crispy all over. With the tongs, transfer the sambuus from the oil to the paper towel–lined plate. Repeat until all the sambuus have been fried. Serve hot with basbaas on the side.

Nafaqo (a word that means "nutritious") is a fried snack similar to a Scotch egg. But instead of a hard-boiled egg encrusted in meat, nafaqo pads the egg with thick mashed potato that is dipped in a bright-orange batter and fried until crisp. Nafaqo is often served as a snack alongside sambuus and bajiye. This recipe calls for cutting the boiled eggs in half for smaller nafaqo, but you can also keep the eggs whole, as is traditional.

There are versions of nafaqo made without eggs, using just small pieces of boiled potato or sweet potato dipped in batter. While the bright-orange batter is a distinctive feature of nafaqo, some cooks dip the potato-encrusted egg into an egg wash and coat it with breadcrumbs before frying it. However you enjoy nafaqo, don't forget to serve it with condiments: A little basbaas or leeleefow makes this snack sublime.

Nafaqo *(POTATO SCOTCH EGG)*

MAKES 10

5 large eggs

3 large russet potatoes (about 3 pounds / 1.4 kg total), scrubbed

1 teaspoon Vegeta seasoning (see page 48)

¾ cup (95 g) all-purpose flour

⅔ cup (160 ml) cold water

3 tablespoons cornstarch

⅛ teaspoon powdered orange food coloring

⅛ teaspoon powdered yellow food coloring

Vegetable or canola oil, for frying

Basbaas (page 63) or Leeleefow (page 75), for serving

Fill two separate pots with water and bring to a boil over high heat. Adjust the heat to medium-high and boil the eggs in one pot and the potatoes in the other. Boil the eggs for 10 minutes and the potatoes for 30 minutes, until they are easily pierced with a fork. Drain each as they finish cooking; let everything cool a bit, and peel both the eggs and potatoes.

Cut the eggs in half and place the halves on a plate; set aside. In a medium bowl, mash the potatoes and allow them to cool until they're still warm. Mix the Vegeta seasoning into the mashed potatoes. Set aside.

In a medium bowl, mix together the flour, water, cornstarch, and orange and yellow food coloring until a thick orange batter forms. Set aside.

Take one egg half and, with your hands, mold mashed potato around it until it is completely covered in a potato layer without any of the egg showing. Smooth the surface with your hands. Dip the potato-encrusted egg into the orange batter until it's coated all over; set gently on a plate. Repeat with the remaining egg halves.

Line a plate or colander with layers of paper towel and set beside the stove. Pour 1 to 2 inches (2.5 to 5 cm) of oil into a pot or deep skillet and heat over medium-high heat until the oil is shimmering and loose. Carefully lower the nafaqo into the oil one or two at a time, making sure they are not touching, and fry for 2 minutes per side, until the batter has fried into a crisp outer shell. Transfer the finished nafaqo to the paper towel–lined plate or colander and repeat until all nafaqo have been fried. Serve immediately with basbaas or leeleefow, and enjoy.

SABIIB RESTAURANT

In the Acton neighborhood of West London, there is a beautifully decorated Somali restaurant called Sabiib. Before you set foot inside, the sign tells you what awaits: "Sabiib: Somali Food Made with Love." Inside, the smells of traditional Somali spices and the sounds of old-school qaraami music hang in the air, transporting each customer to owner Liban Tahlil's beloved homeland.

Born in Mogadishu in 1977, Liban is the son of educators. He had an immensely happy childhood, full of food and love. He had many sisters and often found himself close to the kitchen—more interested in food than most young boys are. His extended family gathered at his home every Friday, as is customary, to enjoy large meals together.

On occasion, his family would host a martiqaad, larger gatherings of guests where they would serve special martiqaad food: big platters of bariis and hilib (rice and meat), freshly caught and fried whole fishes, traditional breads like muufo, and plates of sweets. This style of Somali food remains Liban's favorite, and it's the basis of the menu at Sabiib. Liban also recalls fond memories of visiting the famous Caffè Nazionale with his father, feasting on fluffy brioche as his father drank coffee with colleagues. His appreciation for restaurant culture was nurtured by his father, who loved taking him to nicer restaurants in Mogadishu where they might dine alfresco on fresh fish and pasta.

Gloom slowly crept into this beautiful life. Residents of Mogadishu heard about clashes throughout the country, and family members began showing up at Liban's home seeking sanctuary from the violence. One day in 1991, while a fourteen-year-old Liban was sitting for his year-eight exam, the halcyon days of his childhood came to an abrupt end when gunshots rang out from Mogadishu's city center. This was the sound of his whole world changing forever. Classes were dismissed abruptly, and the school shut down. Liban walked home amidst growing chaos, with police and military forces filling the streets. War had broken out.

Liban's family relocated to the city of Jowhar until the active fighting in Mogadishu calmed down. They returned to Mogadishu after the fall of Siad Barre, and many of them remain there to this day. However, not everyone stayed. Liban's older siblings emigrated to Europe, and Liban himself bounced around between Kenya, Ethiopia, and Somalia before finally leaving for London in September of 1995, over his father's protests.

When eighteen-year-old Liban arrived in London, he was on his own, as his siblings had settled in Sweden. He lived in a homeless hostel in the posh Kensington area until 1998. He enrolled in college and began working at gas stations, graduating and finding his own apartment in 1999. Once he had a home of his own, he began learning how to cook both British and Somali foods, experimenting and watching cooking programs on British television. Soon after, he got married. Children and successful business ventures followed, and in 2014 he ventured into the culinary space via an incredibly successful and lucrative Mexican-themed halal burger chain called Habanero's, which would last for ten years.

Despite monetary success, Liban found himself unsatisfied. On a trip to Nairobi to see his father, he began eating his way through the local food scene—and noticed how Somali restaurants in particular were thriving. Once he was back in London, a dinner at Dishoom (an iconic group of vibrant, Bombay-style cafés) inspired him to ask himself: What if I could make a Somali version—a restaurant that prioritized martiqaad, or hospitality culture?

In 2019, Liban began working on the menu and the business plan for what would become Sabiib. The 2020 pandemic brought all his planning to a halt, and he found himself at home like everyone else, cooking his way through the lockdown. But there was a silver lining: The delivery business at Habanero's exploded during lockdown, a success that would later finance the launch of Sabiib.

In 2022, he found a venue for the new restaurant, and his wife came up with the name Sabiib, which means "raisin" in Somali. The timing was good: When lockdown was lifted, people were eager to dine in again and, as it happened, they were interested in Somali cuisine. Sabiib was an instant success. Liban feels that this is a pivotal time for Somali food in London, and clearly it's easy to love Somali food, as evidenced by the twelve thousand covers a month that Sabiib continues to maintain. The most frequent diners are first-, second-, and third-generation Somali emigrés eager for a more upscale dining experience and thrilled to see their culture reflected back to them in the London food scene.

Building on the success of Sabiib, Liban has opened a second Sabiib location in North London and is also developing a fast-casual Somali concept called Jiko ("kitchen" in Somali). Both are sure to be exciting developments for Sabiib's loyal customers.

These black-eyed pea fritters are similar to falafel and are a favorite afternoon snack. Black-eyed peas are soaked overnight and then blended with chiles, garlic, cilantro, and onion; this mixture is formed into balls, fried, and served hot. Bajiye is typically eaten during casariyo, or afternoon tea, but it's also a popular street food served alongside sambuus, nafaqo, and condiments like leeleefow; it also makes an appearance on Somali tables during Ramadan. Dip bajiye into both leeleefow and basbaas for a sweet and spicy treat.

Bajiye *(BLACK-EYED PEA FRITTERS)*

MAKES ABOUT 55 (1-INCH / 2.5 CM) FRITTERS

2 cups (335 g) dried black-eyed peas

¼ red onion, coarsely chopped

4 garlic cloves, smashed

2 fresh red Thai chiles

⅔ cup (10 g) cilantro leaves and tender stems

¼ cup (60 ml) water

1½ teaspoons salt

Vegetable or canola oil, for frying

Basbaas (page 64), for serving

Leeleefow (page 75), for serving (optional)

Soak the black-eyed peas in water to cover overnight; the peas' outer skins will detach and rise to the surface as they soak. When you are ready to make the bajiye, discard the soaking water and the outer skins, making sure to rub off any still-attached skins.

Combine the black-eyed peas, onion, garlic, chiles, cilantro, water, and salt in a blender and blend into a thick, smooth paste. Let sit for 30 minutes before frying.

Add 2 inches (5 cm) of oil to a large, deep frying pan and heat over medium-high until the oil is hot but not smoking. Place a paper towel–lined baking sheet next to the stove. Scoop up rounded teaspoons of the dough, form into small, rounded disks, and slide into the oil. Fry in batches, with plenty of space between the bajiye, for a little under 1 minute on the first side and 30 seconds on the second side, until brown on both sides. With a slotted spoon, remove the fried bajiye to the paper towel–lined baking sheet. Repeat until all the batter has been used, making sure to maintain the oil's temperature. Serve immediately with basbaas and, if you like, leeleefow.

Bur, sweet cardamom beignets, are found on Somali tables during Ramadan and at other times of celebration. The bur is related to the mandazi eaten throughout East Africa but differs in that it is made using whole-milk powder instead of coconut milk. In the diaspora, Nido powdered milk is standard, and it's widely available in halal or Somali stores as well as online; you can, however, substitute another whole-milk powder as needed. During Ramadan, Somalis like to split a bur in half, stuff a piece of sambuus inside, and enjoy this sweet-and-savory combination. You can also enjoy it on its own with a strong cup of milky shaah (tea).

Bur *(CARDAMOM BEIGNETS)*

MAKES 16 BUR

- ½ cup (120 ml) warm water
- ½ cup (100 g) sugar
- ½ teaspoon instant dry yeast
- 2¼ cups (288 g) all-purpose flour, plus more as needed
- 1 large egg, beaten
- 1½ teaspoons powdered whole milk (preferably Nido brand)
- ¾ teaspoon ground cardamom
- ½ teaspoon salt
- Canola oil, for oiling the dough and frying

In a large bowl, mix together the water, sugar, and yeast and set aside for 10 minutes, until foamy. Add the flour, egg, milk, cardamom, and salt and mix with your hands until a cohesive dough forms. Knead the dough in the bowl for 6 minutes, until smooth. Drizzle the dough lightly with 1 teaspoon of oil and rub it all over to coat. Return the dough to the bowl and cover with a kitchen towel. Let it rise in a warm place until it doubles in size, about 2 hours.

Divide the dough in half. Keep one half in the bowl and transfer the other half to a floured work surface. Roll out the dough into a circular shape about 10 inches (25 cm) wide and ½ inch (1.3 cm) thick. Using a knife, cut the dough into quarters, and then cut each quarter in half so you have eight equal wedges; set these aside and repeat the process with the remaining dough.

Set a paper towel–lined baking sheet next to the stove. In a large skillet, heat 1 inch (2.5 cm) of oil over medium heat until it's loose and hot but not smoking. Slide in the dough pieces three or four at a time (so each has plenty of room), and fry for 30 seconds to 1 minute per side, turning the bur with a slotted spoon or tongs. Once each bur is a deep golden brown on all sides, transfer it to the paper towel–lined baking sheet to cool. Repeat the process until all the bur have been fried. The bur should be eaten as soon as they are cool enough to handle.

These small rounded doughnuts can be found in various forms in many African countries, each with its own approach. Bur kuus kuus, whose name translates roughly to "a pastry that is round," is a beloved Ramadan snack. While you are perfectly welcome to enjoy it unadorned, some families go an extra step, drizzling bur kuus kuus with simple syrup or sweetened condensed milk. Whichever option you choose, these small round bur are a lovely treat, and perfect with a cup of qaxwo (coffee).

Bur Kuus Kuus *(SMALL ROUND BEIGNETS)*

MAKES ABOUT 25

⅔ cup (160 ml) warm water

2 tablespoons sugar

1 teaspoon active dry yeast

2 cups (260 g) all-purpose flour

1 large egg, beaten

¼ teaspoon salt

2 tablespoons canola oil, plus more for frying

Sweetened condensed milk, for serving (optional)

In a large bowl, mix together the water, sugar, and yeast and set aside for 10 minutes, until foamy. Add the flour, egg, oil, and salt and mix with a spoon until a cohesive dough forms. Knead the dough in the bowl for 5 minutes, cover the bowl with a towel, and set aside to rise, about 1 hour. The dough should double in size and be dense and moist inside.

Line a plate or colander with paper towels and set it beside the stove. Place a deep skillet over medium heat and add 1 inch (2.5 cm) of oil; heat the oil until it's shimmering. Wet your hands with water and push down the dough. Grab a handful of dough, and as you close your fist around the dough, form a ring with your thumb and index finger. As you hold your hand over the pot, squeeze a ball of dough through that ring and cut the dough off with a spoon, letting it drop carefully into the hot oil. Continue to add rings of dough to the oil, giving each plenty of space to fry. Cook the balls for 1 minute per side, until they are golden brown all around. As they're done, remove the fried bur to the paper towel–lined plate or colander. Repeat this process with the remaining dough.

To serve, transfer all the hot fried bur to a large bowl and, if you like, drizzle them with sweetened condensed milk, sweetening them to your taste. Serve immediately.

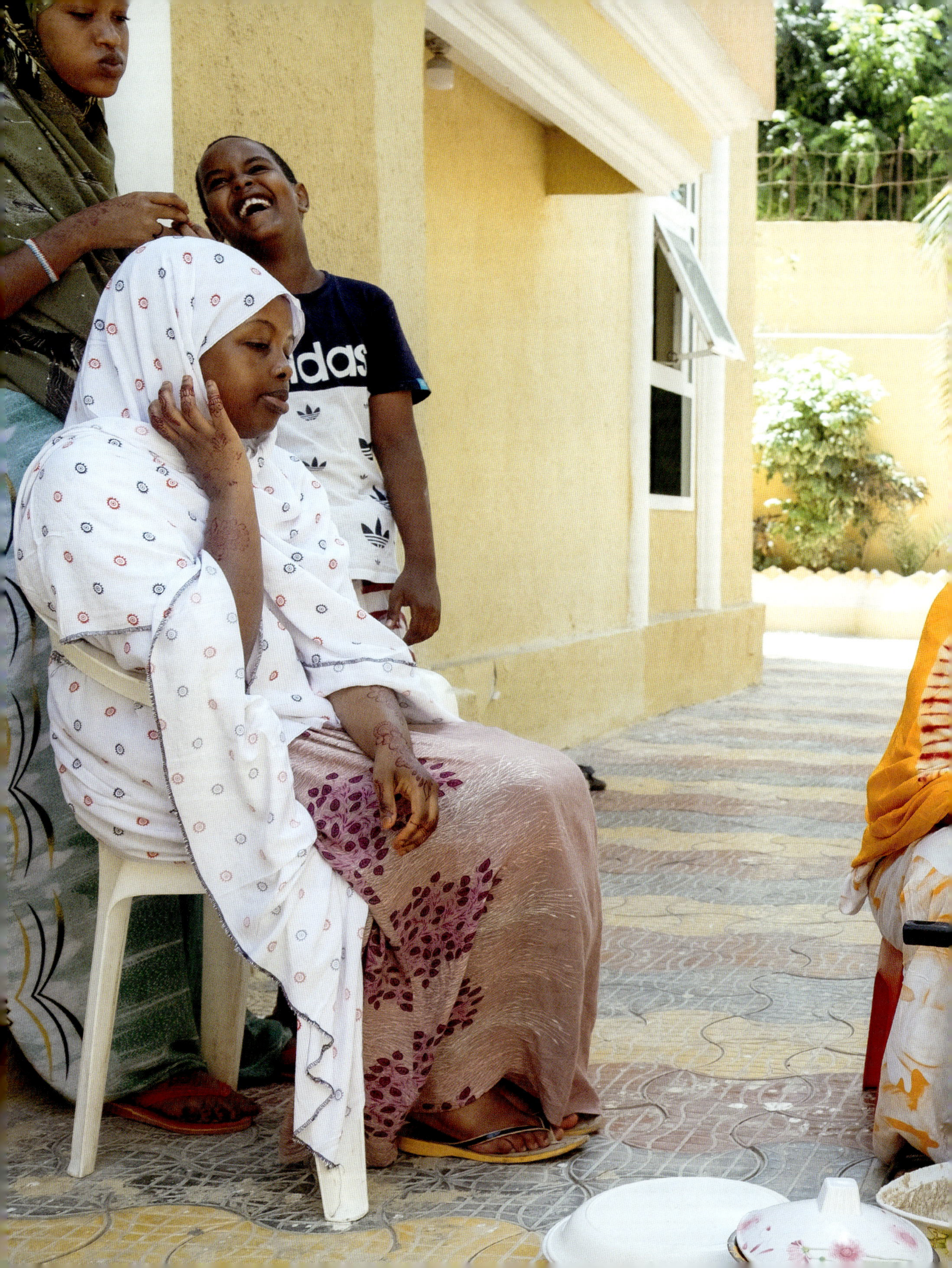

Mango and papaya are just two of the many tropical fruits found in abundance in Somalia. This simple salad is typically served as a refreshing dessert alongside other sweets. In my childhood home, it was served when guests came over for a martiqaad, or hospitable gathering, and during Ramadan. Picking perfectly ripe fruit can be tricky, but it's essential for this fruit salad; choose mangoes and papaya with flesh that is fragrant and soft to the bite but still holds its shape when sliced. Taste the fruit and, if it isn't sweet enough, stir in a half teaspoon of sugar; this will nicely balance the lime juice. Chill the fruits in the fridge prior to cutting for a more refreshing salad.

Cambe iyo Babaay *(MANGO AND PAPAYA)*

SERVES 3 TO 4

2 large chilled ripe mangoes, peeled and sliced

1 large chilled ripe papaya, peeled, seeded, and sliced

1 lime, halved

½ teaspoon sugar, or to taste (optional)

Combine the mango and papaya in a large bowl and squeeze the lime halves over the fruit. Taste and, if needed, stir in the sugar. Serve immediately.

CHAPTER 6

Light Bites

Cambuulo—adzuki beans—is one of the most traditional of Somali foods, and it carries much cultural pride and significance. It dates from ancient times—it's a food our ancestors ate before colonization, particularly in the more southern regions of Somalia. Cambuulo is usually eaten for dinner, served with sesame oil drizzled on top and a little sugar for sweetness; here it is paired with rice, but white corn, among many other foods, can accompany it. Bun has many cultural and religious functions: Somalis use it to welcome guests, and rub it into the skin of expectant mothers. It is traditional to fry the beans in oil and then place them with the oil in a wooden container called a kurbin, which is then passed around so everyone can smell the fragrance of the bun. Then the coffee beans are chewed and the oil is placed in one's palms to rub into hair, hands, and face.

Cambuulo iyo Bun

(SWEET ADZUKI BEANS WITH FRIED COFFEE BEANS)

SERVES 6 TO 8

1½ cups (295 g) dried adzuki beans

7 cups (1.7 L) water

½ teaspoon salt

½ cup (100 g) basmati rice, rinsed clean

⅔ cup (160 ml) untoasted sesame oil, for frying

1 ounce (30 g) whole coffee beans

Sugar, to taste

In a large pot over medium-high heat, combine the adzuki beans, water, and salt. Bring to a boil and cook, uncovered, at a medium boil for 55 minutes. Add the rice, lower the heat to medium, cover, and cook for 1 hour and 15 minutes, until the beans are tender and the liquid is gone.

While the cambuulo cooks, place the sesame oil in a small pot over medium heat. When the oil is shimmering, add the whole coffee beans and fry them, stirring occasionally to keep them from burning, until they're fragrant, about 2 minutes. Take the pot off the heat and allow it to cool. Take a little of the oil and rub it into your palms. Dole out spoonfuls of the bun (coffee beans) and a little oil over the cambuulo and serve, making sure to sprinkle with sugar to taste. Reserve any leftover oil for future use.

In Somali culture, it is customary not only to follow Halal dietary restrictions but also to observe certain eating practices, including hand washing. When receiving guests, Somalis bring a bowl of water called a farxal for hand cleansing. As a form of blessing before eating or drinking, one must say "Bismillah" (in the name of Allah) and then only eat with their right hand as is Sunnah.

Fuul is the Somali version of the dish called ful medames, which is eaten throughout North Africa, East Africa, and the Middle East. Preparation methods for this dish vary from country to country, and the Somali version is made by mashing fava beans and simmering them in a fragrant tomato-cilantro-garlic sauce. Xawaash adds spice and a bit of heat, and makes this a distinctly Somali take on a transregional classic. Fuul is a favorite breakfast in many households; serve it alongside eggs and fresh canjeero (page 80)—the perfect vehicle to scoop up the beans. While this is a breakfast staple, it can be eaten anytime, ladled over bariis cad (Somali-style white rice) and accompanied with basbaas.

Fuul *(FAVA BEAN STEW)*

SERVES 4

2 tablespoons olive oil

1 medium yellow onion, finely diced

6 garlic cloves, minced or crushed

4 large tomatoes, coarsely chopped

1 (14-ounce / 395 g) can small fava beans, rinsed and very well smashed

1½ tablespoons Xawaash (page 56)

1 teaspoon fine sea salt

1 cup (16 g) coarsely chopped cilantro leaves

1 cup (240 ml) water

¼ cup (60 ml) tomato sauce

In a deep skillet or pot over medium heat, heat the oil for about 1 minute, until loose. Add the onion and cook, stirring occasionally, until soft, 5 to 6 minutes. Add the garlic and tomatoes, cover, and cook for 8 minutes or until the tomatoes have softened.

Add the mashed fava beans, xawaash, and salt to the pot; stir to combine and cook for 1 minute, then add the cilantro, water, and tomato sauce. Cover the pan, turn the heat to medium-low, and simmer for about 15 minutes, stirring occasionally, until the beans and tomatoes have incorporated into a thick stew. Add a bit of water if you find that the fuul has gotten too thick, and serve.

EVC PLUS
610 91 11 16

This hearty and delicious vegetarian soup has a few different names, including the Arabic shurbo cadas. While *digir* is the generic word for beans in Somali, and *maraq digir* translates to "bean soup," this soup is specifically made of lentils (misir). Alongside the lentils are carrot, onion, and tomato, but the real star of this soup is xawaash: The classic spice mix transforms it from just any lentil soup to a warming, flavorful, distinctly Somali lentil soup. Maraq misir is frequently made during Ramadan and served as a light starter for the iftar, or fast-breaking meal. It freezes very well and can be eaten on its own or served with bread or rice.

Maraq Misir *(LENTIL SOUP)*

SERVES 4 TO 6

2 tablespoons olive oil

1 medium yellow onion, finely diced

3 medium tomatoes, chopped

4 cups (960 ml) water

1 cup (200 g) red lentils, rinsed

1 small carrot, peeled and finely diced

⅔ cup (10 g) cilantro leaves, finely chopped

4 garlic cloves, smashed or minced

1½ tablespoons Xawaash (page 56)

1½ teaspoons fine sea salt

Bread or rice, for serving (optional)

Heat the oil in a medium pot over medium-high heat for about 1 minute, until shimmering. Add the onion and cook for 8 minutes, stirring occasionally, until it has softened and begun to look translucent. Add the tomatoes, cover, and cook for 6 minutes, until the tomatoes are breaking down.

Add the water, lentils, carrot, cilantro, garlic, xawaash, and salt. Cover and cook over medium heat for 25 minutes, stirring every once in a while, until the vegetables have softened into the soup. If you prefer a smooth soup, purée in a blender, working in batches if you need to. Serve with bread or rice or on its own.

These slightly sweet, fluffy corn muufo (also known as Bravanese bread) come from Baraawe, a city in southwestern Somalia, where the dough is steamed and baked in a traditional clay oven. You will need to use an oven-safe metal wok (or a deep metal frying pan with high, sloping sides): The balls of muufo dough are placed in a circle inside the rim of a hot pan and slowly slide down as they cook in the steam that they release. Serve muufo Baraawe fresh and hot with a stew or soup, and keep any leftovers stored where it will not dry out; it will keep for two to three days.

Muufo Baraawe *(CORN ROLLS)*

MAKES 8 ROLLS

- 2¼ cups (256 g) white corn flour
- ¼ cup (50 g) sugar
- 1 tablespoon active dry yeast
- 3½ cups (830 ml) warm water, divided
- 3½ cups (530 g) all-purpose flour
- ½ teaspoon salt
- ½ teaspoon baking powder
- 1 tablespoon canola oil

In a large bowl, combine the corn flour, sugar, and yeast and add 1½ cups (360 ml) of the water; mix to combine. Set aside for 15 minutes to allow the yeast to activate.

Add the all-purpose flour, salt, baking powder, and remaining 2 cups (470 ml) water to the bowl with the yeast mixture; stir to combine into a wet dough. Cover the bowl with a kitchen towel and set aside in a warm place for 2 hours to allow the dough to rise.

Preheat the oven to 400°F (200°C). In a large deep oven-safe non-stick wok, heat the oil over medium-high heat. The muufo dough will be very soft and sticky, so wet your hands when you work with it. Grab an eighth of the dough, mold it into a rounded shape, and place it inside the rim of the wok. It will slowly slide toward the center of the wok. Working quickly, form seven more dough balls, placing each next to the last in a circular pattern around the perimeter of the wok. (If the wok doesn't fit all the pieces of dough, make two batches of four.) Turn off the burner, cover the wok tightly with a lid, and place the wok in the oven and cook for 30 minutes. Do not remove the lid, as the muufo need the steam in order to cook all the way through. Remove the pot from the oven and take off the lid. With a spatula, transfer the muufo to a serving platter and serve right away.

ABDISALAN WARSAME, ON CAMEL HERDING

The United Nations declared 2024 the Year of the Camel, highlighting the importance of camels to the economies and cultures of ninety countries and to the livelihood of millions of people. The UN also called for more investment in camel husbandry, in recognition of the camel's potential to help advance the United Nations' Sustainable Development Goals, which are aimed at fighting poverty and hunger.

Somalia, which is said to have the largest number of camels of any country, holds camels in high esteem. They are a status symbol, a working asset, and a form of currency. Camels are woven deeply into the fabric of Somali culture, featuring in poetry and music and touching everything from language and literature to the law.

Not surprisingly, there are many famous Somali proverbs that highlight camels' importance to Somali society. Among these are *Aakhiro nimaan geel lahayn, lama amaan-ayne* (A man without a camel is not praised in the afterlife) and *Geel nin aan lahayn, geeridii war ma leh* (The death of a man with no camels is no news).

The value of camels to the Somali people is something that Abdisalan Warsame, professor at Somali National University, knows quite a lot about. Long before he was a professor of economics and management science, he was a young camel herder. He was born in the Galgaduud region of Somalia in 1987 to a family that split its time between the small town where his mother lived and the capital city, Mogadishu, where his father and older siblings spent most of their time. As the youngest sibling, Abdisalan stayed with his mother in the country, tending to the family's livestock.

As he grew older, he took turns with his older siblings—spending time in the city to attend school, and alternating with periods in the country herding camels and later caring for the family's farmland. The camels, a present from his paternal grandfather to his sons, were quite literally the family's livelihood: As Abdisalan puts it, "In rural areas, if you don't have camels, you don't have wealth."

Herding runs in both sides of his family: His mother grew up as a camel herder, a role girls—particularly eldest daughters—may occupy in rural areas. Learning begins early in nomadic families, and a young Abdisalan often accompanied his older siblings as they worked. It's not uncommon for children as young as five to begin herding duties; often they are paired with older camels that have a bell (koor) around their neck that helps locate them in the event they get lost.

The rules and expectations of camel-herding culture don't necessarily match those of city life. Communities are tightly knit; it's expected that people will take care of one another. And herders know the members of their flocks intimately—quite literally down to their footprints.

This way of life is rapidly changing as more herders leave for cities with camels in tow, as industrialization reduces the grazing and roaming lands of the quiet and freedom-loving camel. Young people, often descended from generations of nomadic herders, are increasingly fleeing rural areas for safety from groups like fundamentalist militia al-Shabaab or for economic opportunities. Often without formal education, varied work experience, or contacts who can line up work for them, young rural-born Somalis can find it difficult to survive in major cities. Abdisalan credits his ability to move between a rural nomadic life herding camels and an urban life attending school largely to his family having a foot in both worlds. Many other herders are not so lucky.

The uptick in herders relocating to cities has resulted in a decrease in the number of small-scale camel owners and a rise in industrial camel farming, with an overall negative impact on Indigenous foodways, the national economy, and Somali culture as a whole. Abdisalan shares that, in the Dayniile area, large-scale industrialized camel farms keep the camels caged in specific areas—something unimaginable in the past. The camel milk market (an estimated $7.5 billion globally in 2023) is booming in Somalia, even as demand for camel meat itself is falling.

The move from rural areas to cities is profoundly impacting agriculture as a whole. Camel herders, like their farmer counterparts, encounter safety and security issues, with al-Shabaab controlling many rural areas—and the agricultural output from those areas. As a result, local production of Indigenous foods decreases, along with knowledge of practices like livestock herding: No one is there to do that work. This situation has paved the way for processed and imported foods' becoming a larger part of many Somalis' diets.

Abdisalan describes the herder diet as something that once was hyperlocal. People in rural areas once relied almost entirely on food that was sown and harvested, foraged, or raised and slaughtered by them. Diets varied depending on where one lived, but herders once largely lived on milk, meat, foraged seeds and fruits, and the occasional measure of bartered grain. Rural diets and city diets were so different that those living in the country would often get sick when they came to cities. Today, most

Somalis' diets are virtually the same, with everyone increasingly reliant on processed and imported foods.

Livestock is one of Somalia's most important exports, and herders' abandoning rural life in the same way as their farmer counterparts poses a real threat to the country's GDP. Yet there is no systematic data collection from the government to indicate how the sector has been impacted, making the way forward obscure.

Camels are no longer the status signifier they once were, and consumption of camel meat is no longer associated with higher class or wealth, as wealthy locals and diaspora returnees have influenced local food trends toward seafood and lamb. At the same time, interest in Indigenous foods like camel milk, or cambuulo, is spreading—a resurgence that ironically coincides with declining production of Indigenous foods and an increased reliance on foreign imports.

The way Abdisalan sees it, a few key things need to be done to protect herders, chief among them a stronger national government with control of all of the country's regions. Without a strong government, groups like al-Shabaab will continue to purposely keep people in rural areas hungry, scared, and desperate in order to either recruit them or drive them away from their homes. Al-Shabaab currently makes more money from taxing Somalis than the national government does. If al-Shabaab is eradicated, Abdisalan argues, the government could begin offering programs and funding to support herders and the livestock sector as a whole. As it stands, Somalia's camel culture and economy remain at risk.

For this hearty soup, oats simmer in a spiced goat broth with cilantro and tender chunks of goat meat. It's a favorite Ramadan dish as the oats are a slow-release carbohydrate that keeps a person fueled over time. This soup can be blended (with the meat removed before blending and then added back in), but it's also wonderful as an unblended soup.

Shurbad *(GOAT AND OAT PORRIDGE)*

SERVES 4 TO 6

- 1 pound (455 g) bone-in goat meat cubes
- 10 cups (2.4 L) water
- 1 cup (85 g) rolled oats
- 1 tablespoon Vegeta seasoning (see page 48)
- 2 teaspoons Xawaash (page 56)
- 1½ teaspoon salt
- 2 tablespoons olive oil, divided
- ½ medium white onion, minced
- 2 large tomatoes, chopped small
- 4 garlic cloves, smashed
- ⅔ cup (10 g) coarsely chopped cilantro leaves
- 1 teaspoon tomato paste
- ¼ teaspoon ground black pepper
- lime slices, for serving

In a large pot, add the goat meat and the water and bring the water to a boil. Once the meat has been boiling for 15 minutes, skim any impurities that have made it to the top with a spoon.

Next, add in the oats, Vegeta, xawaash and salt. Turn down the heat to medium, and cover and cook for an hour.

While the meat cooks, add 1 tablespoon of the oil to a large non-stick skillet and warm over medium-high heat. Once the oil is loose and shimmering, about one minute, add in the onions, cover with a lid, and lower the heat to medium. Cook the onions until they have softened, about ten minutes. Stir as needed.

Add in the tomatoes and the remaining tablespoon of oil and cover, making sure to stir occasionally. Cook until the onions break down, about 15 minutes.

In a mortar and pestle, pound the garlic and cilantro and mix it into to the tomato mixture and cook for five minutes.

Transfer the tomatoes to the pot with the goat meat. Add in a teaspoon of tomato paste and black pepper and cook covered for 1 hour and 10 minutes, stirring as needed. Once the goat meat is tender and the oats have thickened, take the pot off the stove and serve with a squeeze of lime.

While rice and pasta have become the most common starchy foods in the Somali diet, corn dates back to precolonial times. Ground corn, or grits (soor), remains a staple in agricultural areas today as a go-to lunch for workers. It's very filling, and it's a perfect canvas for whatever you'd like to serve it with—whether that's stew, soup, or a simple topping of buttermilk and sugar. While it shares some similarities with Kenyan ugali, soor's texture is a bit looser. What follows is a basic recipe for soor, but there are many variations. Soor furfur is grits made with a broth or sauce, in a method that cooks the grain kernels separately. Soor can also be made from sorghum instead of corn. If you're eating soor with a savory topping, make sure to add a little basbaas (page 63), which will push it from simple comfort food to something special.

Soor *(CORN GRITS)*

SERVES 4

3½ cups (840 ml) cold water

1 teaspoon fine sea salt

1 cup (125 g) fine white cornmeal

In a medium pot over medium-high heat, combine the water and salt and bring to a boil. Slowly add in the cornmeal, whisking continuously as the soor thickens, 7 to 8 minutes.

Lower the heat to medium-low, cover, and cook, stirring occasionally, for about 25 more minutes, until thick with no sign of grittiness. If the soor begins sticking, add a splash of water. Once it is creamy, take the pot off the burner. Serve hot.

Maraq ari is the king of Somali soups and easily the most well known. It can be enjoyed on its own or as part of a simple lunch with fresh muufo (page 135). Maraq ari broth is also the flavorful base for many Somali rice dishes. A close cousin of this soup, maraq fahfah includes more vegetables, such as cabbage, carrots, and potatoes. You can vary the vegetables to your liking, but always include the garlic, onion, cilantro, and spices, which in addition to the umami from the Vegeta are the blueprint for the flavor in this soup.

Maraq Ari *(SPICED GOAT SOUP)*

SERVES 6

1 pound (450 g) bone-in goat meat, cut into cubes

6 cups (1.4 L) water

1 medium white onion, coarsely chopped

5 garlic cloves, smashed

1 tablespoon Vegeta seasoning (see page 48)

1 tablespoon ground cumin

1 teaspoon whole coriander seeds

¼ teaspoon ground black pepper

1 medium Russet potato, peeled and cut into chunks (optional)

¾ cup (12 g) coarsely chopped cilantro leaves and tender stems

Soor (page 140) or fresh bread, for serving (optional)

Preheat the oven to 400°F (200°C).

Rinse the goat meat under running water and place it in a large oven-safe pot with a tight-fitting lid. Add the water, onion, garlic, Vegeta seasoning, cumin, coriander, and black pepper and cover the pot with the lid.

Place the pot in the oven and cook for 2 hours, then add the potato, if using, and cilantro to the pot. Replace the lid and cook for another 30 minutes, or until the meat is fork tender and the potatoes are soft. Remove from the oven and use a slotted spoon or tongs to remove the potato chunks and pieces of goat meat from the soup; set these aside. Using a fine-mesh strainer, strain the broth into serving bowls; discard the strained-out solids. Add chunks of potato (if any) and goat meat to each serving and enjoy the soup on its own or with bread or soor.

In restaurants, you are much more likely to find maraq ari (goat soup; page 143) than you are maraq digaag, which is a beloved staple of Somali home cooking. This flavorful soup offers a great deal of comfort; the potatoes give it body while the xawaash and jalapeño give it a hint of heat. It is the perfect soup to make when a loved one is ill and in need of an extra bit of nourishment. Enjoy the soup on its own or serve it with bread, rice, or a little pasta such as orzo.

Maraq Digaag *(CHICKEN SOUP)*

SERVES 6

2 tablespoons olive oil

1 medium red onion, diced

3 medium tomatoes, diced

1½ pounds (680 g) boneless, skinless chicken thighs

Juice of ½ lemon

2 teaspoons fine sea salt

3 cups (720 ml) water

1 cup (16 g) loosely packed coarsely chopped cilantro leaves and tender stems

1 small carrot, diced

1 jalapeño, halved lengthwise

6 garlic cloves, minced

1½ tablespoons Xawaash (page 56)

1 medium russet potato, peeled and cut into ½-inch (1.2 cm) cubes

In a large pot over medium heat, heat the oil until it shimmers and add the onion. Cook for 6 minutes, stirring a few times, until the onions have softened but are not fully translucent. Add the tomatoes, stir, cover the pot, and cook until the tomatoes begin to break down, about another 6 minutes.

Meanwhile, place the chicken thighs, lemon juice, and half the salt in a medium bowl; mix to coat the chicken and let it marinate for a few minutes. Make space in the middle of the tomatoes and add the chicken thighs to the pot. Turn up the heat to medium-high and sear the chicken for about 2 minutes on each side.

Add the water, cilantro, carrot, jalapeño, garlic, xawaash, and remaining 1 teaspoon salt. Bring to a simmer, cover, reduce the heat to medium-low, and cook for 13 minutes, until the carrots have softened slightly. Add the potato and cook, covered, stirring occasionally, for 20 more minutes, until the potato is tender; serve.

This corn flatbread is a beloved symbol of Somali cuisine. In Mogadishu, there are entire restaurants that sell only muufo and maraq (soup). In these restaurants you tear up pieces of muufo, then ladle over brothy maraq ari (goat soup) and drizzle with a little sesame oil. You can also use muufo as the basis for a sweet dish: Tear pieces, soak them in shaah (spiced tea), and serve with mashed banana and a drizzle of sesame oil or subag (ghee). It's not uncommon for a xaafad (neighborhood) to have one lady who makes and sells muufo for everyone. Customers can see her making the muufo traditionally in a tinaar (tandoor oven) and are able to buy the most freshly baked muufo. In the diaspora, where people usually do not have access to a tinaar, muufo is often pan-fried, as it is in this recipe.

Muufo *(CORN FLATBREAD)*

MAKES 8 FLATBREADS

3½ cups (448 g) all-purpose flour

1 cup (135 g) pre-cooked fine white cornmeal

4 tablespoons (50 g) sugar

2 teaspoons active dry yeast

1 teaspoon fine sea salt

3 cups (720 ml) water

4 tablespoons (60 ml) olive oil

In a large bowl, mix together the flour, cornmeal, sugar, yeast, salt, and water. Knead until the ingredients bind together into a sticky dough. Cover the bowl with a kitchen towel and let rise in a warm place for 1 hour.

Fill a small bowl with water and place the olive oil in another small bowl; set these and the bowl of dough next to the stove, along with a teaspoon and a brush or paper towel to use with the oil. In a 10-inch (25 cm) nonstick skillet, heat 1 teaspoon of the oil over medium-high heat, swirling it over the base of the pan. When the oil is hot but not smoking, wet your fingertips in the bowl of water and grab a little over 1 cup (240 ml) of dough. Place it in the hot skillet. With wet fingers, quickly begin to spread the dough outward from the center into a rounded shape about 7 inches (18 cm) wide. Cover the pan immediately and cook the muufo until the bottom is brown in color and you hear a sizzling sound, about 2 minutes.

Remove the lid, brush the muufo lightly with olive oil, and flip it over. Cook the second side uncovered until the muufo loses its doughiness, 2 or 3 minutes. Transfer to a plate and follow the same steps until you have a stack of eight fluffy muufo. Muufo is best eaten hot, so enjoy right away.

JAMAL HASHI, CHEF

In 2022, Apple TV+ premiered an episode of the newest season of its show *Little America*. That episode focuses on a Somali American chef debuting "camel on a stick" at the Minnesota State Fair. In the episode, the chef breaks a rib, faints from exhaustion, and his restaurant floods, all before he can make his debut. Despite these extreme challenges, he successfully introduces camel-meat kebabs and wins over the fair's attendees. This episode is based on the real-life experience of Somali American chef Jamal Hashi; the experience launched Jamal into local fame, and his culinary star only rose from there.

Before Hollywood came calling, Jamal was a young boy in Mogadishu. Born in 1982 as the fifteenth of seventeen children, Jamal had a blissful childhood. His home was always full of relatives, friends, and neighbors, all coming together over large platters of delicious home-cooked food. In particular, he has tender memories of his patriotic father, a former revolutionary, born in 1921, who took part in the overthrow of the colonial regime.

Jamal's earliest food experiences centered around his family. His father was an avid cook who loved making seafood dishes for his children. So despite the kitchen being the domain of women and girls in Somali culture, Jamal is not the first male cook in his family, though he is the first trained chef. He fondly describes the mango trees in his family's yard and the taste of his first lobster, prepared by his father. These experiences among many others planted the seeds of his future as a chef.

As he describes it, this idyllic childhood came to an end in 1991, when the Somali Civil War reached him. On an otherwise normal day in Mogadishu, eight-year-old Jamal and his brother were swallowed by a crowd of people coming from the direction of their home. Deducing that these people were running from some kind of violence, the boys fled for their lives as well. While this may have saved them, it also severed them from their family; soon they were on a boat to Kenya. They would not be reunited with family until 1992, when they met some of their family members at the Utange refugee camp. They learned that Jamal's beloved father had passed away and that some of his older siblings had fled to Europe and the United States. In 1993, when he was ten years old, Jamal followed them, landing in Washington, DC, where he was met by some of his older siblings and several aunts. Three years passed before Jamal moved to Minneapolis; he finished his schooling there.

While studying business administration, Jamal began working at an Italian restaurant as a dishwasher; he was also helping out at his mother's restaurant, one of the first Somali restaurants in Minnesota—a state that now has one of the largest Somali populations outside of Somalia. He fell in love with the restaurant industry, but his family didn't approve of it as a career path for him. To appease them, he began attending both culinary school and real estate school in 2005. He never got around to getting his real estate license, but he did become part owner of his family's restaurant.

In 2006, he created his own off-shoot restaurant called Safari Express: It was the first fast-casual African restaurant in the United States. He created unique menus that made Somali food accessible to everyone, even vegetarians. Soon, he was a fixture in the Minnesota food scene, entering cooking competitions and making appearances on local TV. It was around this time that camel meat became newly available in the US, and Jamal debuted it at the Minnesota State Fair in 2010. He went on to open several more restaurants, including Safari in 2015, alongside Mona Birjeeb (it was the first Somali restaurant in New York City).

Today, Jamal works as a culinary consultant all over the US, including for Saint Paul Restaurant and Catering, the largest minority-owned catering company in the country. The company produces food for about fifteen schools and thirty mosques and churches, serving thirteen thousand meals per day. Jamal's continuing importance to Somali food in the US cannot be overstated.

Sabaayad is a cousin of Kenyan chapati and Indian paratha. Its ingredients are simple, but the trick for truly tender sabaayad is in the technique—letting it rest for just the right amount of time and really working the dough to achieve the multiple layers.

Sabaayad can be eaten for lunch with stews and other savory foods or enjoyed on its own at breakfast time or as a snack, along with a cup of sweet shaah (spiced tea). The Somali American diaspora also uses sabaayad in a delicious dish called kay kay: Invented nearly thirty years ago, it consists of torn-up sabaayad mixed with proteins like beef, goat, or chicken, and with vegetables. While this sabaayad is made with all-purpose flour, sorghum flour is traditional.

Sabaayad *(FLAKY PAN-FRIED FLATBREAD)*

MAKES 6 FLATBREADS

2¾ cups (352 g) all-purpose flour, plus more for dusting

1 cup (240 ml) hot water

¼ cup (60 ml) canola oil, plus more as needed

2 teaspoons sugar

½ teaspoon salt

Combine all the ingredients in a large mixing bowl and knead until a sticky dough forms; continue kneading and working the dough until it is smooth, about 5 minutes. Cover the bowl with a kitchen towel and let the dough rest in a warm place for 2 hours.

Generously flour a work surface and a rolling pin. Divide the dough into six equal balls. Roll one ball out into a square shape with the rolling pin. With your fingertips, lightly rub the surface of the dough with a little oil. Fold the dough square in half, then fold in half again over itself. Set the folded dough aside and repeat the process with the remaining five pieces of dough. Let the folded pieces rest for 45 minutes.

With a floured rolling pin, roll out a piece of folded dough on a floured work surface into an 8-by-9-inch (20 by 23 cm) square. Set it aside on a greased counter space or parchment-lined baking sheet. Repeat with the remaining pieces of folded dough.

Set a large plate next to the stove. Using a paper towel, grease a large skillet or pan with canola oil and set it over medium-high heat. Once the oil is hot but not smoking, lower the heat to medium and place one piece of rolled-out dough on it. Cook the sabaayad for 1 to 2 minutes, until golden-brown pockets form all over the bottom. Drizzle oil on the uncooked side and flip the sabaayad

over; cook the second side for 1 minute, then transfer the sabaayad to the plate. Repeat the process with all the remaining pieces of rolled-out dough, greasing the pan in between batches as needed. Cover the cooked sabaayad to keep it from drying out. Serve warm.

This homey vegetarian spinach stew is often confused with koosto, a stew made with Swiss chard. Cagaar (*ah-gaar*), also known as bukurey, can be served with canjeero (page 80), rice, or soor (page 140), typically at lunchtime. While this recipe calls for frozen spinach, wild or cultivated raw spinach is more traditional. If you want more than a small hit of heat, use more jalapeño pepper to your taste.

Cagaar *(SPINACH-TOMATO STEW)*

SERVES 4

- 2 tablespoons olive oil
- 1 large red onion, diced
- 6 garlic cloves, minced
- 5 medium tomatoes, diced
- 1 (16-ounce / 450 g) bag frozen cut spinach
- 1½ cups (360 ml) water
- ¾ cup (12 g) coarsely chopped cilantro leaves
- 2 tablespoons Xawaash (page 56)
- 1¾ teaspoons fine sea salt
- 1½ tablespoons tomato paste
- 1 medium jalapeño, halved

In a medium pot, heat the oil over medium-high heat for 1 minute or until shimmering, then add the onion. Cook, stirring a few times, until the onion has softened, about 5 minutes. Stir in the garlic and tomatoes and cook over medium heat, covered, until the tomatoes are beginning to break down, another 5 minutes.

Add the spinach, water, cilantro, xawaash, salt, tomato paste, and jalapeño. Cover and cook the cagaar for 20 minutes, stirring occasionally, until the tomatoes have cooked down, the spinach is a darker green, and the onions are soft. Serve immediately atop soor.

The name of this tomato sauce roughly translates to "cheap and easy." Thanks to its humble ingredients—cilantro, garlic, onions—dallac bilaash carries a lot of flavor. But the real star is the jalapeño pepper, whose touch of spice takes this dish to the next level. Dallac bilaash can be paired with soor or bread, but it's revelatory when tossed with fresh pasta and served alongside thinly sliced busteeki (page 169) and salad. Keep your dallac bilaash covered as you cook so as to retain as much moisture as possible.

Dallac Bilaash *(CILANTRO AND GARLIC TOMATO SAUCE)*

SERVES 4

2½ tablespoons olive oil

1 large red onion, halved and sliced

6 garlic cloves, peeled

1 cup (16 g) cilantro leaves, finely chopped

5 large tomatoes, coarsely chopped

1 medium jalapeño, halved

½ green bell pepper, sliced

2½ teaspoons Vegeta seasoning (see page 48)

In a pot over medium-high heat, heat the oil until shimmering; add the onion and cook for 5 minutes, stirring a few times, until the onion has softened significantly. Meanwhile, smash the garlic and cilantro together in a mortar and pestle until a thick paste forms.

Stir in the tomatoes and jalapeño, cover, and cook for 10 minutes, occasionally lifting the lid and mashing the tomatoes, until the tomatoes have cooked down to a thicker, cohesive consistency. Add the cilantro and garlic, the bell pepper, and the Vegeta. Stir together and cover, reduce the heat to medium, and cook for 15 minutes, until the peppers have softened slightly. Serve.

This earthy and flavorful vegetarian dish can be served as a side to meats and starches. While people sometimes mistranslate *koosto* as "spinach," the heart of this dish is definitely Swiss chard. This recipe pairs koosto with baamiye (okra), and features tomato, onion, garlic, and cilantro in supporting roles. Feel free to customize the dish by adding more vegetables, like cabbage or carrots. Serve for lunch or as a light dinner with soor (page 140), rice, or a flatbread like sabaayad (page 150).

Koosto iyo Baamiye *(SWISS CHARD AND OKRA STEW)*

SERVES 3

¼ cup (60 ml) olive oil

½ red onion, diced

8 large okra pods, stemmed and sliced

4 large tomatoes, diced

1 tablespoon Vegeta seasoning (see page 48)

¾ cup (12 g) cilantro leaves, coarsely chopped

6 garlic cloves, smashed

2 bunches Swiss chard, leafy part and midrib coarsely chopped

½ cup (120 ml) water

In a medium pot over medium-high heat, heat the oil for 1 minute. Add the onions and cook for 4 minutes, then add the okra and cook for another 3 minutes, stirring occasionally, until everything has softened slightly. Add the tomatoes and Vegeta seasoning; stir, cover, and cook for 10 minutes, until the tomatoes are broken down and begin to thicken.

Add the cilantro, garlic, Swiss chard, and water to the pot, cover, and cook over medium heat for 30 minutes, until the Swiss chard turns a darker green, the okra is tender, and a little liquid remains in the pot.

CHAPTER 7

Mains

Baasto, or pasta, is Somalia's clearest culinary relic from the era of Italian colonization. While it is eaten throughout the country, its stronghold is in the south, in what was once Italian Somaliland (see page 28). The earliest import of pasta to Somalia dates to the late 1800s, when Italians began establishing their colonial rule. With our embrace of pasta, Somalis have taken a food that symbolized colonial oppression and claimed it on our own terms: Somali pasta dishes use Somali spices and are quite distinct from Italian preparations. Several different suugos, or sauces, exist; this one has potato and ground beef as its foundation, with the potato binding the dish into a delicious whole. Spaghetti, macaroni, or penne would all pair well with this suugo.

Baasto iyo Suugo Hilib Shiishiid *(PASTA WITH MEAT SAUCE)*

SERVES 6

3 tablespoons olive oil

1 medium white onion, diced

½ pound (225 g) ground beef

1 medium russet potato, peeled and chopped

6 garlic cloves, pounded

2 tablespoons ground cumin

1½ teaspoons fine sea salt

½ teaspoon Vegeta seasoning (see page 48)

¾ cup (12 g) finely chopped cilantro leaves

6 medium ripe tomatoes, diced

1 cup (240 ml) water

6 tablespoons (100 g) tomato paste

1 green bell pepper, sliced

1 pound (450 g) pasta

In a medium pot over medium-high heat, heat the oil until shimmering, about 1 minute. Add the onion, cover, and cook until it's slightly softened, 4 to 5 minutes. Add the ground beef, breaking up any chunks. Cook uncovered, stirring occasionally, until browned, 3 to 4 minutes. Add the potato, garlic, cumin, salt, and Vegeta seasoning and cook, stirring occasionally, for 7 to 8 minutes.

Meanwhile, combine half the cilantro, the tomatoes, and the water in a blender; purée until smooth. Add this mixture to the pot, then stir in the tomato paste and the remaining chopped cilantro. Reduce the heat to medium-low, cover, and cook for 35 minutes while stirring occasionally. When the suugo has 15 to 20 minutes left, add the bell pepper and start cooking your pasta in a separate pot.

When it's ready, the suugo will be thickened significantly, with small pools of oil at the top, and the bell pepper will have softened—for firmer peppers, take the pot off the stove a few minutes earlier. Serve hot, tossed with the cooked pasta.

This suugo says so much about Somali culinary history. The pasta is a relic of colonialism, while the tuna reflects Somalia's long coastline and seafood-rich waters. Xawaash, the spice mix shaped by Somalia's centuries-long trading history along the Indian Ocean's spice routes, ties it all together. Even the words for tuna, *tuuna* and *toonno*, are borrowed from English and Italian. Rich as it is with history, this is an exceedingly simple dish that comes together easily; it's a little less rich than other suugos since it uses fish instead of meat, but it is in no way light on flavor.

Baasto iyo Suugo Tuuna *(PASTA WITH TUNA SAUCE)*

SERVES 4 TO 6

2 tablespoons olive oil

1 medium red onion, diced

6 garlic cloves, smashed

1 (5-ounce / 142 g) can yellowfin tuna in olive oil (not drained)

½ cup (8 g) coarsely chopped cilantro leaves

2 tablespoons Xawaash (page 56)

¾ teaspoon fine sea salt

¼ teaspoon ground black pepper

1 (24-ounce / 680 g) jar good-quality marinara sauce, such as Rao's

1 pound (450 g) spaghetti

In a medium skillet, heat the oil over medium-high heat until shimmering, then add the onion and cook, stirring occasionally, for 7 minutes, until no longer firm. Next, stir in the garlic and cook for 1 minute, being careful not to let it burn.

Add the tuna and its oil, along with the cilantro, xawaash, salt, and black pepper. Cook for 2 minutes, then add the marinara, stir to combine, and cover the pan. Turn the heat down and let the sauce simmer, stirring occasionally, while you cook the pasta.

Before you drain the pasta, add a little pasta water to the sauce to loosen it if needed. Drain the pasta, combine it with the sauce, and serve.

MOGADISHU

Somali-style lasagna is a great example of how Somalis have reimagined Italian dishes. The sauce is Somali-style suugo, with herbs and spices like cilantro and cumin and a combination of fresh tomatoes and jarred store-bought marinara. You can use whatever cheese you'd prefer or have on hand: While mozzarella and parmesan are classic, in Somali American diasporic communities, Mexican cheese blends are popular. This baasto is wonderful for feeding a crowd—perhaps at your next *martiqaad*.

Baasto Lisaanyo *(SOMALI LASAGNA)*

SERVES 6 TO 8

- ⅓ cup (80 ml) olive oil, plus a drizzle for the pasta water
- 1 small red onion, diced
- 1 pound (450 g) ground beef
- 1 teaspoon salt, plus more for the pasta water
- ½ teaspoon ground cumin
- 1½ cups (360 ml) water
- ¾ cup (12 g) cilantro leaves, finely chopped
- 15 garlic cloves, minced or smashed
- 3 tomatoes, diced
- 1 (28-ounce / 790 g) jar good-quality marinara sauce, such as Rao's
- 1 pound (450 g) lasagna noodles
- 20 ounces (570 g) cheddar-jack cheese, shredded

In a medium pot over medium-high heat, heat the oil until it's loose; add the onion and cook for 5 minutes, until it softens. Add the beef and stir to break up any clumps. Once the beef has begun to brown slightly, about 2 minutes, stir in the 1 teaspoon of salt and the cumin and cook, stirring often, for 9 minutes, until all the liquid has evaporated. Combine the water, cilantro, garlic, and tomatoes in a blender and pulse until smooth. Add this liquid to the meat. Cook for an additional 10 minutes, then add in the marinara sauce and cook for another 30 minutes, stirring occasionally, until little pools of oil surface to the top of the sauce.

While the sauce cooks, preheat the oven to 350°F (180°C) and cook the lasagna noodles according to the package instructions. Strain the noodles and run cold water over them briefly to help them cool a bit.

In the bottom of a deep 9-by-13-inch (23 by 33 cm) baking dish, spread one-fifth of the tomato sauce at the bottom. Cover with a layer of lasagna noodles, then top with another one-fifth of the sauce and one-quarter of the cheese. Repeat until all the noodles, sauce, and cheese are used.

Cover the lasagna with aluminum foil and bake for 30 minutes, or until all the cheese has melted. For the last 5 minutes, remove the aluminum foil so the cheese on top of the lasagna can get slightly crispy and golden brown. Remove the lasagna from the oven and let it cool a bit before serving.

This dish is known by several names: kalamuudo, galamuddo, garamuddo. It's a dish from the Banaadiri community that spread to other parts of southern Somalia, but it isn't widely known outside the region. Chunks of goat meat are cooked in tomato sauce until tender, and then fresh hand-rolled noodles are cooked in the meaty broth. Given the fresh pasta element, this dish is a time commitment, but it's well worth the effort. Serve with the coconut hot sauce, basbaas qumbe (page 72).

Kalamuudo *(HANDMADE PASTA WITH GOAT RAGÙ)*

SERVES 8

For the Sauce

10 garlic cloves, minced or smashed

2 cups (32 g) loosely packed cilantro leaves and tender stems

5⅓ cups (560 ml) water

½ cup (120 ml) olive oil

½ medium red onion, diced

¼ cup (60 g) tomato paste

1 tablespoon Xawaash (page 56)

6 medium tomatoes, diced

2 pounds (910 g) bone-in goat meat, cut into 8 to 10 medium-sized pieces

3 tablespoons Vegeta seasoning (see page 48)

For the Pasta

3 cups (385 g) all-purpose flour

2 large eggs

½ cup (120 ml) water

1 tablespoon vegetable oil

¾ teaspoon salt

To Serve

Basbaas Qumbe (page 72)

To make the sauce, combine the garlic, cilantro, and ⅓ cup (80 ml) of the water in a blender and blend until smooth. Next, warm the olive oil in a large pot over medium-high heat until it's shimmering. Add the onion and cook, stirring, until it begins to soften, about 7 minutes. Stir in the tomato paste, cilantro-garlic purée, and xawaash, and cook for 5 minutes more.

Combine the tomatoes and 1 cup (240 ml) of the water in the blender and purée until smooth. Add the puréed tomatoes to the pot and cook for 10 minutes, until the sauce is darker in color and slightly thicker. Add the meat, another 1 cup (240 ml) of water, and the Vegeta seasoning. Cover and cook over medium heat until the meat is tender, about 1 hour.

While the sauce is cooking, make the pasta. In a bowl with a beater, or in the bowl of a stand mixer, combine the flour, eggs, water, oil, and salt and mix until a rough dough forms. Knead the dough by hand for 5 minutes, until smooth, then divide it into two balls.

Take one ball of dough and roll on a floured surface into a rough 10½-inch (27 cm) square. Cover the other ball so it doesn't dry out as you work on the first half. With a sharp knife or pizza wheel, cut the dough into three equal sections, each about 3½ inches (9 cm) wide, trimming the square as needed for straighter edges. Working with one section at a time, cut smaller pieces that are 3½ inches

Recipe continues

(9 cm) long and ½ inch (1.3 cm) wide. Continue cutting until the three sections of dough have been transformed into a mountain of thin strands of pasta. Dust the pasta with a scant amount of flour and roll each piece, one by one, between your palms or on the work surface until they are no longer flat; as you finish each, place them on a sheet pan. Repeat the whole process with the other ball of dough. Let the pasta dry for at least 30 minutes and up to 1 hour.

When the meat is tender, add the remaining 3 cups (720 ml) of water to the sauce and bring to a gentle boil over medium-high heat. Turn the heat to medium-low, add all the pasta, and cook for 20 minutes, stirring only once or twice.

Take the kalamuudo off the stove and serve immediately with the chunks of tender bone-in goat and basbaas qumbe to pass around the table. Make sure each person has meat on their plate and they can discard the bones after.

Busteeki—thinly sliced steak cooked simply with cilantro, tomatoes, garlic, onion, and spices—is typically served for lunch atop plates of steaming pasta with dallac bilaash (tomato sauce; page 153). This flavorful dish relies on just a few ingredients and offers a big return on flavor. It can also be paired with a flatbread, like muufo (page 147), or with rice, a salad, and basbaas. Store any leftovers in an airtight container in the fridge for up to three days.

Busteeki *(STEAK)*

SERVES 4 TO 5

6 garlic cloves, minced or smashed

1½ cups (24 g) coarsely chopped cilantro

¼ cup (60 ml) water

⅓ cup (80 ml) olive oil

1½ pounds (680 g) boneless top round beef steak, sliced ½ inch (1.3 cm) thick

1¼ tablespoons Vegeta seasoning (see page 48)

1 tablespoon ground black pepper

½ red onion, thinly sliced

1 large tomato, sliced

In a blender, purée the garlic, cilantro, and water until smooth; set aside. In your largest skillet, heat the oil over medium-high heat until it's loose. Place the steak slices in the skillet in a single layer; if you run out of room before you run out of steak, work in batches. Cook the steak for 4 minutes in the hot oil, turning the pieces after 2 minutes. Return all the steak to the pan (if necessary) and add the Vegeta seasoning, pepper, onion, and tomato to the pan and mix everything together.

Once the tomatoes have begun to break down, 5 to 7 minutes, add the puréed garlic-cilantro mixture. Cover the pan, lower the heat to medium, and cook for 30 minutes, stirring occasionally to make sure the meat is not sticking to the bottom of the pan. Serve right away.

When the topic turns to Somali rice, this fragrant spiced rice pilaf is where my mind goes. Every household has its own way of making bariis. However, some things are law, such as always rinsing your rice until the water runs clear, always soaking your basmati rice, and always using spices (cumin, cardamom, cinnamon, black pepper). Other things are optional, such as which food coloring to use. Food coloring itself is what makes Somali rice so recognizable, and it's usually orange, but red and (very rarely) green are also possibilities. Some people use liquid saffron for the vibrant orange streaks; others use orange food dye. Other rice toppings can include sautéed onions, peppers, and sweet raisins. This pilaf is typically eaten at lunchtime with meat, chicken, or fish, along with salad and basbaas—and, always, a banana.

Bariis *(RICE PILAF)*

SERVES 6 TO 8

For the Rice

2 cups (400 g) basmati rice

⅔ cup (10 g) cilantro leaves

¼ cup (60 ml) room-temperature water, plus 1 teaspoon (for the food coloring)

4 garlic cloves, minced or smashed

2 tablespoons olive oil

1 medium red onion, diced

5 green cardamom pods

1 teaspoon cumin seeds

½ teaspoon whole black peppercorns

1 whole cinnamon stick

2½ chicken bouillon cubes (preferably Maggi brand; see page 48)

3⅔ cups (880 ml) boiling water

½ teaspoon fine sea salt

½ teaspoon orange food coloring (optional)

For the Potato

1 large russet potato, peeled and cut into fries ½ inch (1.3 cm) thick

½ teaspoon fine sea salt, plus more if needed

½ teaspoon water

⅛ teaspoon orange food coloring

Vegetable or canola oil, for frying

Wash the rice in cold water until the water is clear. Soak the rinsed rice in clear, cold water for 1 hour; drain and set aside.

Preheat the oven to 350°F (180°C). Purée the cilantro, ¼ cup (60 ml) water, and garlic in a blender until smooth; set aside.

Heat the olive oil in a large ovenproof pot over medium-high heat. Once the oil is loose, add the onion and cook for 5 minutes, until soft with light browning on the edges. Add the cardamom, cumin, peppercorns, and cinnamon, and stir for 1 to 2 minutes, until fragrant. Add the bouillon cubes to the pot and dissolve, then add the garlic-cilantro purée. Add the rice and allow the mixture to cook down for 1 minute. Add the 3⅔ cups boiling water and salt, increase the heat, and bring the rice to a boil. Stir well, then cover the pot and transfer it to the bottom rack of the oven to bake for 20 minutes or until the rice is tender and fluffy.

While the rice bakes, put the potato into a bowl and sprinkle it with salt. In a small bowl, mix the water and food coloring and pour this over the potato, mixing with a spoon so your hands don't stain.

Add ½ inch (1.3 cm) of oil to a medium frying pan over medium-high heat. Line a plate with paper towels and put it next to the stove. Once the oil is shimmering hot, fry the potatoes until crispy, stirring occasionally, about 15 minutes. Remove the fries from the pan and place them on the paper towel–lined plate to drain.

Remove the rice from the oven. If you like, mix the ½ teaspoon of orange food coloring with the remaining teaspoon of water and drizzle this over the rice. Let the rice cool, fluff it with a fork, and serve with the fries on the side.

This dish is a childhood favorite of mine—and it offers a big reward for minimal effort. Goat is a lean meat and it can take a while to cook until it's tender, so you'll want to start cooking at least ninety minutes before you plan to serve it. It makes a delicious main course for six or eight; serve it with basbaas cagaaroo la tumay (page 64), banana, and limes.

Bariis Isku Karis *(ONE-POT GOAT AND RICE)*

SERVES 6 TO 8

3 cups (600 g) basmati rice

1½ cups (24 g) loosely packed cilantro leaves, finely chopped

2 tablespoons ground cumin

12 garlic cloves, minced or smashed

⅓ cup (80 ml) olive oil

2½ pounds (1.1 kg) bone-in goat meat, cut into 8 to 10 pieces

½ medium red onion, diced

4 teaspoons salt

5 large tomatoes, chopped

7 cups (1.7 L) water

Rinse the rice in cold water until the water runs clear. Pound the cilantro, cumin, and garlic into a rough paste in a mortar and pestle.

In a large ovenproof pot over high heat, heat the oil until it's shimmering. Add the goat meat, onion, and salt and cook, stirring occasionally, until the goat is browned, about 1 minute. Stir in the tomatoes and cilantro-cumin-garlic paste. Turn the heat down to medium-high, cover, and cook for another 35 to 38 minutes, until the tomatoes have begun to cook down.

Uncover the pot, add the water, and cook until the liquid is very hot and steaming and the goat is more tender, about another 10 minutes. Meanwhile, preheat the oven to 400°F (200°C).

Add the rice to the pot and bring the liquid to a boil over high heat. Cover the pot and place it in the oven for 35 minutes. In the final 7 minutes of cooking time, set the oven to broil (low) and cook the covered rice, checking frequently to make sure it does not burn. When the rice has absorbed all the water and is cooked all the way through, take the pot out of the oven, fluff the rice with a fork, and serve.

This fluffy white rice is cooked in chicken bouillon with classic Somali flavors: garlic, onions, cardamom, and cumin. It's a simpler dish than bariis isku karis (page 173) but still has a deep, comforting flavor. It's also made with jasmine rice, whose grains are thicker than the more customary basmati rice. This dish is perfect paired with a vegetable side like koosto (Swiss chard) and a saucy main dish like mallaay qumbe (page 177), or it can be eaten on its own—perhaps by small children who may not like the black peppercorns and food coloring in the classic bariis.

Bariis Cad *(SPICED WHITE RICE)*

SERVES 6

- 2 tablespoons vegetable oil
- ½ small red onion, diced small
- 4 garlic cloves, smashed
- 6 whole green cardamom pods
- 1 teaspoon ground cumin
- 2 chicken bouillon cubes (preferably Maggi brand; see page 48)
- 6⅓ cups (1.5 L) boiling water
- 3 cups (600 g) jasmine rice, well rinsed

Preheat the oven to 400°F (200°C).

Heat the oil in a medium-to-large ovenproof pot over medium-high heat for 1 minute, then add the onion and cook until softened, about 5 minutes.

Add the smashed garlic and cook, stirring, for a minute or two, then stir in the cardamom pods, cumin, and bouillon cubes, mashing them with a spoon as they cook. When the spices are fragrant, pour in the boiling water. Allow the spices to steep for 3 minutes, then add the rice and bring back to a boil. Boil for 4 to 5 minutes, then cover the pot and transfer it to the oven for 30 minutes, until all the liquid is absorbed and the rice is tender. Remove the pot from the oven and fluff the rice with a fork, then serve.

Despite Somalia's long coastline, seafood has not traditionally been a big part of the Somali diet outside of coastal towns. In most of the country, red meat has been king, and both seafood and poultry have been seen as lower-class food, or not "real" food, in comparison to red meat. In the 1970s and 1980s, in a time of severe famine, the government tried to combat the negative view of seafood and boost the fishing sector. They relocated nomads to fishing cooperatives and even made certain days of the week officially "meat-free" days, dedicated to seafood consumption. Despite these efforts, the industry did not take off. A decade later, the Somali Civil War saw the full collapse of this sector. More recently, interest in seafood consumption is growing.

Mallaay qumbe can be found up and down the East African coast, including in the coastal towns of southern Somalia. This version is distinctly Somali, due to the addition of xawaash and creamy coconut milk. Serve mallaay qumbe with rice or soor (page 140).

Mallaay Qumbe *(COCONUT FISH CURRY)*

SERVES 4

1¼ teaspoons fine sea salt

1 pound (450 g) barramundi or other firm white fish, cut into serving-size pieces

2 tablespoons olive oil

1 medium red onion, diced

2 large Roma tomatoes, finely diced

8 garlic cloves, minced

1 (13½-ounce / 400 ml) can unsweetened coconut milk

1 cup (16 g) cilantro leaves, finely chopped, plus more to serve

4 teaspoons Xawaash (page 56)

Steamed white rice, for serving

Sprinkle ¼ teaspoon of the salt over the fish; put it aside.

In a pot just large enough to accommodate the fish in one layer, heat the oil over medium-high heat. Once the oil is hot but not smoking, add the onion and cook, stirring, for 8 to 10 minutes, until almost translucent. Add the tomatoes, cover, and cook for 7 minutes, occasionally stirring and smashing the tomatoes down as they cook.

Add the garlic and cook for a minute or two, then add the coconut milk, cilantro, xawaash, and the remaining 1 teaspoon salt; stir and cover. Cook for 4 minutes to allow the flavors to come together, then add the fish, making sure the coconut milk covers the fish (if necessary, add a splash of water to cover). Cover and cook for 8 to 10 minutes, until the fish can be easily flaked with a fork. Serve the curry with rice, topped with additional chopped cilantro.

THE SOMALI FISHING INDUSTRY

One of the most potent—though quite recent—stereotypes of Somalis is that of the Somali pirate. This trope emerged in the 2000s and 2010s due to a rise in incidents off the Somali coast; however, labeling these events simply as acts of piracy is too simplistic an explanation of a complex issue.

The phenomenon of the Somali pirate (burcad badeed) and, more broadly, the issues facing Somali fishermen are issues Dr. Abdiaziz Hussein Hassan, associate professor at Somali National University, knows well. Born in Hargeisa in 1984 and raised in Mogadishu, Dr. Hassan has worked with Somalia's ministries of fisheries and ports for years. He also works with the Food and Agricultural Organization of the United Nations on improving fish quality and production for, and implementing market standardization in, the Somali fish market. Over the phone, Dr. Hassan described to me what the Somali fishing industry was before the Somali Civil War—and long before Hollywood depicted Somali fishermen as pirates.

Despite Somalia's having the longest coastline in mainland Africa, seafood has not been a food staple for most of the population, the exception being those living in coastal fishing towns. Broadly, Somalis consider red meat to be the best meat one can consume and fish to be a lower-status food. To combat these attitudes, the Somali government started a series of campaigns between 1969 and 1991 to promote fish consumption and to help build the Somali fishing industry. In 1974, the government promoted the formation of fishing cooperatives, and by 1979 there were eighteen. Cooperatives sold their fish fresh at local markets, and what could not be sold was salted and sold off to the government-owned and Soviet-funded SOMALFISH. In the mid-1970s, additional fishing settlements were established along the coast for fifteen thousand nomads suffering from that year's drought. The government attempted to train them as fishermen, but by 1979, some abandoned the fisheries and relocated. Dr. Hassan explains that, in the 1980s in particular, the Siad Barre regime implemented a policy in major cities like Mogadishu whereby, for two days each week, only fish could be consumed, and the slaughter of other meat was not allowed. The government hoped this would help stimulate the fishing industry and lead to the creation of fishing jobs.

However, by the end of the 1980s, Somalia was undergoing political instability, and by 1991 had descended into full-scale civil war. Any progress that had been made toward building out the fishing sector ended with the dissolution of the centralized government. This left a great opportunity for anyone wanting to take advantage of the chaos. Foreign countries took this as carte blanche to overfish Somali waters illegally without any governmental authority or coast guard to reprimand or punish them. A free-for-all ensued. It is estimated that foreign vessels went from taking 16,500 tons of fish in 1950 to illegally taking 127,800 tons by 2015, with most of this increase happening during the Somali Civil War.

The illegal fishing done in Somali waters during the war was not the only crisis affecting coastal communities. In 1997, the Italian magazine *Famiglia Cristiana* published an exposé on the illegal dumping of European toxic waste by Italian and Swiss companies in Somali waters; this had begun during the political unrest of the late 1980s. During the Civil War, European companies made arrangements with local warlords to bring weapons and to fish expensive tuna for later sale in exchange for dumping nuclear waste.

In 1994, Italian journalist Ilaria Alpi, who'd been investigating the dumping of toxic waste, was assassinated in Mogadishu alongside her cameraman Miran Hrovatin. According to *The Ecologist*, during the investigation into Alpi's death in 1994, a Somali warlord indicated that she was close to uncovering a "guns-for-waste trade" by the Italian Army and others. Ten years later, containers full of toxic waste washed up on Somalia's shores following a tsunami in Indonesia.

In 2009, Francesco Fonti, an ex-member of the 'Ndrangheta family of the Italian mafia, made a claim that toxic waste had been exported to Somalia under the supervision of Italian politicians and that this was carried out by the crime syndicate while Italian troops on the ground turned a blind eye. He also implicated the United States, Germany, and Russia in the illegal toxic dumping trade and spoke of his experience dumping waste for a Russian businessman close to Vladmir Putin. As a result of the dumping of waste in Somali waters, there was a spike in health issues like cancer, birth defects, and chronic illnesses. The toxic dumping, which was confirmed by the Somali UN envoy Ahmedou Ould-Abdallah in 2008, is ongoing to this day.

It is widely understood that modern Somali "piracy" emerged in response to illegal overfishing by foreign countries, which threatened the economy of coastal fishing communities. Dr. Hassan says that not only were Somali waters being overfished illegally, but often Somali fishermen would set out their nets and return the next day to find that their expensive equipment had been cut or stolen—equipment that many fishermen often borrowed money to purchase in the first place. Illegal fishing, which had started farther off shore, crept closer and closer to the northeastern Somali coast, and locals began dying of malnutrition due to low fish population.

Without a centralized government to protect them and their way of life, Somali fishermen took matters into their own hands, obtaining firearms either from Yemen or from Bakaaro market in Mogadishu. The fishermen initially shot at boats to scare them off, but once the crews on the boats started arming themselves and shooting back, the Somali fishermen began making their way onto the foreign vessels and taking hostages.

Soon, warlords realized that there was money to be made, and they put together unofficial "coast guard" units, utilizing fishermen, local youth, and ex-militia members. It became more profitable to hold people hostage than to fish. They also began to sell illegal fishing licenses to foreign vessels. Several pirate factions were operating simultaneously, not all of them aligned in their goals. In 2008, a Ukrainian ship was captured, and the pirates used the press coverage about the hijacking to bring awareness to the toxic dumping in Somali waters that had ruined the coastline; they asserted their intention of using the $8 million ransom to clean up the waste.

While some have argued that the actions of the pirates brought an influx of cash—and a flashiness—to fishing towns that trickled down to the whole community, others assert that the piracy phenomenon created cycles of violence and spikes in prostitution, inflation, and drug dependency.

Dr. Hassan argues that piracy is also destructive to the overall economy: When locals turned to piracy instead of fishing, it created a general lawlessness throughout Somali waters. Insurance rates for boats going to Somalia tripled, and many avoided Somali waters altogether, taking a longer, alternate route. Prices for imported and exported food and goods also skyrocketed, all of which was detrimental to a nation that is highly reliant on imports.

The chaos of illegal fishing and piracy in Somalia's coastal waters created a storm of destruction for the Somali economy and food system. It also disrupted global trade, amounting to $18 billion in increased trade costs each year. In response to the rise in piracy, the international community launched various initiatives, including the global naval Combined Task Force 151, established in 2009, and the European Union's Operation Atalanta, a naval military counter-piracy initiative off the Horn of Africa.

Japan, India, and the United States also directed patrols in the area, while vessel owners sometimes enlisted private security organizations. The Somali government appealed to the United Nations for help, resulting in several UN resolutions between 2010 and 2022; the Somali government also implemented its own anti-piracy policies. Piracy rates dropped in the years following 2013; however, when UN security measures expired in 2021, piracy once again increased.

Meanwhile, nonprofits like One Earth Future and organizations like the United Nations Food and Agricultural Organization are working to revitalize the Somali fishing industry. These organizations collaborate with local experts like Dr. Hassan to conduct surveys and to train and support fishermen. The Somali government has also been collecting data on fish catch.

Dr. Hassan believes that, for the fortunes of the Somali fishery to change, the industry needs the support of a strong centralized government, standardization and regulation for the industry, better infrastructure and training, and better regional security to stop the continuing theft of Somalia's marine and coastal resources—in particular the fisheries, which author Sarah Glaser estimates to be worth a potential $135 million in the 2015 study *Securing Somali Fisheries*. Somalis are not yet the captains of their own waters, and the challenges remain numerous. But many are working to rebuild and strengthen Somalia's fishing industry and protect its coastal sovereignty. With stronger government action, Somalia and her people could well be on their way to benefiting fully from the rich resources of their own coastal waters.

This hearty, buttery fish dish is modeled after the xawaash-spiced fried fish found on restaurant menus in Mogadishu. You can substitute any other fish with firm white flesh for the barramundi. Frying adds a nice little crust with crispy edges. Serve it with bariis (page 170), salad, and basbaas.

Mallaay Shiilan *(PAN-FRIED FISH WITH XAWAASH)*

SERVES 2 TO 3

- 3 tablespoons olive oil
- 3 garlic cloves, smashed
- 2 teaspoon Xawaash (page 56)
- 1 teaspoon fine sea salt
- ½ teaspoon ground turmeric
- ¼ teaspoon paprika
- ¼ teaspoon ground black pepper
- Juice of ½ lemon
- 2 (12-ounce / 340 g) barramundi fillets (fresh or frozen)
- Canola oil, for frying

If using frozen fish, thaw it overnight in the fridge. Combine the olive oil, garlic, xawaash, salt, turmeric, paprika, pepper, and lemon juice in a large bowl. Rinse the fish under cold water and pat it dry. Add the fish to the marinade, turn it so it's fully coated, then let it sit in the marinade for at least 10 minutes.

Line a plate with layers of paper towel and place it next to the stove. Pour ¼ inch (6 mm) of canola oil into a large, deep skillet. Heat the skillet over high heat until the oil is loose and carefully add the fish. Fry the fish for about 4 to 5 minutes per side (for fillets that are 1½ inches / 4 cm thick; longer if they are thicker), making sure to add oil as needed, until it is no longer raw. Once the fish is crispy and golden on all sides, transfer it to a paper towel–lined plate to cool. Serve hot with rice.

This succulent chicken dish cooks on the stovetop for nearly an hour, until its spices, herbs, and vegetables melt down into a thick sauce. While it can be made with other cuts of chicken, chicken thighs are ideal. Covering the pan as the chicken cooks keeps it nice and juicy. Serve with salad and rice or with a flatbread like sabaayad (page 150) or muufo (page 147).

Digaag *(SPICED CHICKEN)*

SERVES 3 TO 4

1½ pounds (680 g) boneless, skinless chicken thighs

1 lime, halved

⅓ cup (80 ml) olive oil

¼ medium red onion, sliced

1 tablespoon Vegeta seasoning (see page 48)

1 teaspoon cumin

1 teaspoon ground black pepper

½ teaspoon paprika

½ teaspoon red chile flakes

10 garlic cloves, peeled

1 cup (16 g) coarsely chopped cilantro

2 large tomatoes, chopped

Rice, for serving

Place the chicken in a large bowl and squeeze the lime halves over it, turning to coat the pieces in the lime juice.

In a large skillet over medium-high heat, heat the oil until it's loose. Add the chicken and cook for about 5 minutes, until it is browned on both sides, then add the onion, Vegeta, cumin, pepper, paprika, and chile flakes.

Pound the garlic and cilantro into a paste in a mortar and pestle; stir into the pan, add the tomatoes, and cover. Lower the heat to medium-low and cook for an hour, until the chicken is tender. If the chicken is sticking, add a small splash of water. Serve with rice.

Suqaar is a popular lunch staple, and it comes in many forms—camel, chicken, and lamb as well as beef—always with bell peppers and xawaash. When making beef suqaar, choose beef stew meat and cut it into small cubes. Or if you are fortunate enough to be in range of a Somali grocer, look there for precut suqaar meat. Serve hilib suqaar with muufo (page 147) or sabaayad (page 150) or eat it over bariis cad (page 174).

Hilib Suqaar *(BEEF AND VEGETABLE SAUTÉ)*

SERVES 4

2½ tablespoons olive oil

1 large red onion, halved and sliced

1 pound (450 g) boneless beef stew meat, cut into ½-inch (1.3 cm) cubes

2 teaspoons fine sea salt

½ cup (120 ml) water

4½ teaspoons Xawaash (page 56)

7 garlic cloves, minced

1 medium russet potato, peeled and cut into ½-inch (1.3 cm) cubes

½ cup (8 g) coarsely chopped cilantro leaves

1 medium red bell pepper, sliced

1 medium green bell pepper, sliced

In a large skillet over medium heat, heat the oil until it's shimmering. Add the onion and cook for 7 to 10 minutes, stirring occasionally, until no longer firm. Adjust the heat to medium-high, add the meat, and sprinkle over 1 teaspoon of the salt; cook, turning the meat, for about 4 minutes, or until it's browned. Add ¼ cup of the water, the xawaash, and garlic, and cover the pot. Lower the heat to medium and cook for 15 minutes, until the meat is tender.

Add the potato, cilantro, and remaining 1 teaspoon salt; stir, cover, and cook for another 8 to 10 minutes. Add the remaining ¼ cup water and bell peppers, cover, and cook for 15 more minutes, or until the potatoes are tender. Serve hot.

Like all suqaar, this chicken suqaar features xawaash and bright peppers, but it skips the potato found in hilib (beef) suqaar. It has a hint of heat thanks to the black pepper and optional jalapeño. Suqaar is cooked covered to keep the meat juicy and moist. Serve with the flatbread of your choice (canjeero, muufo, or sabaayad) for a light lunch or over plenty of rice for a more filling dinner.

Suqaar Digaag *(CHICKEN AND VEGETABLE SAUTÉ)*

SERVES 4

Juice of ½ lemon

2½ teaspoons Xawaash (page 56)

1 teaspoon fine sea salt

½ teaspoon paprika

⅛ teaspoon ground black pepper

1 pound (450 g) boneless, skinless chicken thighs, cut into bite-sized pieces

2 tablespoons olive oil

1 large yellow onion, halved and sliced

6 garlic cloves, minced

1 medium jalapeño, halved

¾ cup (12 g) coarsely chopped cilantro leaves

1 medium red bell pepper, sliced

1 medium yellow bell pepper, sliced

In a medium bowl, combine the lemon juice, 1 teaspoon of the xawaash, salt, paprika, and pepper. Add the chicken and mix everything together to coat the chicken. Set aside.

In a large skillet over medium-high heat, heat the oil until loose. Add the onion and cook, stirring occasionally, for 8 minutes, or until the onion is softened. Add the garlic and jalapeño and stir for another minute, then add the chicken in a single layer. Allow it to cook undisturbed for 5 minutes, then turn the pieces over and cook for 3 minutes more, until fully cooked through.

Add the remaining 1½ teaspoons xawaash, cilantro, and bell peppers and stir to combine. Cover the skillet and turn the heat down to medium-low; cook until the peppers have softened, 10 to 15 minutes. Serve hot.

Hilib ari and rice is a classic pairing. While camel meat is king, Somalia's abundance of domestic goats means that hilib ari is more readily available (and more affordable) than camel meat. This is especially the case in the diaspora, where goat meat has replaced camel meat as the protein of choice to serve with dishes like bariis (rice pilaf). Due to its leanness, goat meat takes quite a while to cook to tenderness. This recipe gets it there with a combination of oven and stovetop cooking. First the meat is cooked tender in the oven with aromatics, and then it's finished on the stovetop with spices, herbs, and tomatoes that slowly melt into a thick sauce. Precut bone-in goat can be found at most halal butchers and grocery stores and at many mainstream grocers and butchers.

Hilib Ari *(BRAISED GOAT)*

SERVES 5 TO 6

For the Goat

2½ pounds (1.1 kg) bone-in goat meat, cut into medium pieces

3½ cups (840 ml) water

½ medium red onion, sliced

1 cup (16 g) coarsely chopped cilantro leaves and tender stems

1½ tablespoons whole coriander seeds

1 tablespoon Vegeta seasoning (see page 48)

For the Sauce

⅓ cup (80 ml) vegetable oil

¼ medium red onion, sliced

2 large tomatoes, chopped

5 garlic cloves, smashed

½ cup (8 g) coarsely chopped cilantro leaves

1 tablespoon ground cumin

1 tablespoon Xawaash (page 56)

1½ teaspoon salt

Preheat the oven to 400°F (200°C). In an ovenproof pot with a lid, combine the goat meat, water, red onion, cilantro, coriander, and Vegeta seasoning. Cover the pot and place in the oven for 2 hours and 30 minutes, until the goat is aromatic and starting to become tender.

Take the pot out of the oven and remove the cooked goat meat to a dish; reserve. Set a strainer over a bowl and strain the contents of the pot; reserve the broth and discard the strained-out solids.

In a clean pot over medium-high heat, heat the oil until shimmering. Add the sliced red onion and cook for 5 minutes, stirring occasionally, then lower the heat to medium, add the tomatoes and cook, covered, for 10 minutes, until they have broken down.

Pound the garlic, cilantro, and ground cumin together in a mortar and pestle. Add this plus the xawaash to the tomato mixture and stir and cook covered for 15 minutes more. Mix in the reserved goat meat, salt, and 2 tablespoons of the reserved goat broth. Cover and cook over medium-low heat for 1 hour, stirring as needed. During the last 15 minutes of cooking, occasionally check the consistency of the sauce; if it's beginning to stick to the bottom of the pot, add broth 1 tablespoon at a time to deglaze as needed. Transfer the meat to a serving dish and serve.

Somali-style lamb is often braised, and the resulting broth used for rice; it may also be slowly roasted, haniid style, until it's nearly falling off the bone. Either leg or shoulder cuts can be used, but lamb shanks are great in this recipe. The long braise helps achieve tenderness and marries the lamb to a traditional flavor combination of xawaash, cilantro, garlic, and onion. The resulting thick garlicky pan sauce is delicious when sopped up with bariis cad (page 174) or flatbread.

Ido *(BRAISED LAMB)*

SERVES 4

2 lamb shanks or legs (about 2½ pounds / 1.1 kg)

2½ teaspoons fine sea salt

¼ teaspoon ground black pepper

1 tablespoon olive oil

9 cups (2 L) water, plus more as needed

1 large yellow onion, halved and sliced

12 whole garlic cloves, peeled

1 cup (16 g) coarsely chopped cilantro leaves

1½ tablespoons Xawaash (page 56)

Season the lamb with ½ teaspoon of the salt and the ground pepper. In a large pot set over high heat, heat the oil until shimmering. Add the lamb to the pot and sear it on each side until the meat has reached a medium brown, about 1 minute.

Add the water to the pot along with the onion, garlic, cilantro, xawaash, and 1½ teaspoons of the salt. Cover and bring the water to a boil, then turn down the heat to medium and cook at a consistent simmer, covered, for 3 hours, or until the lamb is incredibly tender. Add more water during the cooking time as needed to keep the meat covered.

Transfer the lamb to a serving platter. Turn the heat under the pot back to high, add the remaining ½ teaspoon of salt, and bring the cooking liquid to an aggressive boil. Boil, uncovered, for 10 to 15 minutes, or until the liquid has become a very thick, glossy gravy and the onions have melted. Pour over the lamb and serve.

Dhaylo, or baby goat, is tender, juicy, and flavorful; roasting it yields succulent meat and slightly crisped skin. In Somalia, goat meat has a unique reddish undertone thanks to the yeheb bush goats graze on; a compound in the leaves called cordeauxiaquinone dyes their bones red-pink. The roasting in Somalia is sometimes also done in a cooking pit; here a conventional oven is used. Marinate the goat a day ahead for deeper flavor and keep it covered as it cooks to keep the meat from drying out or burning. Enjoy on a bed of bariis (page 170) and serve with salad and with tamarind basbaas (page 68).

Dhaylo *(ROASTED YOUNG GOAT)*

SERVES 6

½ large red onion, sliced

12 garlic cloves, smashed

1 cup (16 g) coarsely chopped cilantro leaves

⅓ cup (80 ml) olive oil

2 tablespoons Vegeta seasoning (see page 48)

2 tablespoons Xawaash (page 56)

1 teaspoon ground black pepper

Juice of 1 lime

1 to 2 pieces bone-in baby goat shoulder (about 3½ pounds / 1.6 kg total)

1¼ cups (300 ml) water, plus more as needed

Combine the onion, garlic, cilantro, olive oil, Vegeta seasoning, xawaash, pepper, and lime juice in a nonreactive roasting pan, and stir to mix. With a sharp knife, make three or four slits in the goat's skin. Place the goat meat in the pan and turn to coat it thoroughly with the marinade. Cover the pan with aluminum foil and set aside while you preheat the oven. (At this point, you can also marinate the goat overnight in the refrigerator if you like; remove it from the refrigerator half an hour before proceeding, to take off the chill.)

Preheat the oven to 400°F (200°C). Place the foil-covered pan in the oven and bake for 1 hour. Uncover the pan, add the water, and stir it into the marinade. Cover again, lower the heat to 300°F (150°C), and cook the dhaylo for another 1 hour and 25 minutes, or until the meat is extremely tender and brown all over and the vegetables have broken down, turning the meat occasionally and adding more water as needed to keep the marinade from burning or sticking to the bottom.

Remove the dhaylo from the oven and allow it to rest for 5 to 10 minutes before serving.

JUBA FARMS

Brothers Ahmed and Abdiasis Ali grew up in the diaspora, in Kansas and California, hearing stories from their formerly nomadic parents about the importance of camels to the Somali people and culture. Resilient in tough conditions (and a crucial source of food), camels are celebrated in the poetry and music of Somalia—which is also home to the largest number of camels in the world, around 7 million.

Motivated by these stories, the brothers began a search for camel milk dairies in the US so they could gift the milk to their mother and grandmother. When they found an Amish-run camel farm about two hours away from their home in Kansas, they arranged a tour and hit it off with the owner. Over time, they cultivated the relationship, visiting often and learning all they could. Eventually, they negotiated a partnership deal with the farmer: He would continue producing the camel milk, and the brothers would take care of everything from marketing to order fulfillment and delivery.

Their business venture became a success almost immediately thanks to a well-executed social media campaign. The brothers soon had to expand their production

to another camel farm (this one based in Colorado) in order to meet demand. Their loyal customer base includes both nostalgic Somalis in the diaspora and non-Somali Americans (who are about 30 percent of their customer base).

As their success with marketing camel milk grew, the brothers began exploring ways to add camel meat to their product line. The camel population in the US is limited, but the Alis found a solution in Australia, which has plenty of camels (including an overpopulation of feral camels). The brothers reached a sourcing agreement with a company that raises camels and slaughters them in keeping with both Islamic (halal) dietary rules and US (FDA) standards. The camel meat is harvested in Australia, then shipped to a halal processing facility in Chicago before making its way to Juba Farms customers. This new product offering has delighted Somali Americans, who rarely get to enjoy this delicacy in the United States.

As their customer list grows—and with a high demand for camel meat and milk in neighboring Canada—the brothers are making further plans to expand operations. They are particularly focused on their homeland, hoping to partner with (and open markets to) camel herders in Somalia and to continue building a larger camel milk distribution system. With their mission to make camel milk and meat more accessible to a global Somali diaspora, Ahmed and Abdiasis are supporting a pillar of their cultural heritage, one glass of camel milk at a time.

In Somalia, camel meat is a cultural mainstay. Somalis living abroad, however, often lament how difficult it is to find. Camel meat for this recipe can be ordered through Somali groceries or halal butcher shops—with the best cut for this recipe being the outer thigh and hindquarter of the camel. If there are none of these nearby, you can order it online from distributors like Kansas-based Juba Farms (see page 196).

Hilib geel translates to "camel meat," and *kalaankal* refers to the style of this dish. The cubes of meat are cut slightly larger than suqaar cubes, but the dish is cooked a little more simply than hilib suqaar. It lands somewhere between oodkac and suqaar—cooked simply with a few core ingredients, resulting in succulent bites of meat coated in a thick onion-garlic sauce. Serve with a flaky flatbread like sabaayad (page 150), or with canjeero (page 80), for a delicious lunch.

Hilib Geel Kalaankal *(CAMEL COOKED WITH ONION)*

SERVES 4

¼ cup (60 ml) vegetable oil

½ large red onion, sliced

1 pound (450 g) camel meat, cut into 1-inch (2.5 cm) cubes

½ cup (8 g) cilantro leaves, finely chopped (optional)

5 garlic cloves, smashed

1 tablespoon Vegeta seasoning (see page 48)

1 tablespoon ground cumin

1 cup (240 ml) boiling water

In a medium pot over medium heat, heat the oil until shimmering. Add the onion to the pot and cook for 10 minutes until very soft. Adjust the heat to medium-high, add the camel meat, and cover. Cook for 4 or 5 minutes, stirring a few times so the meat sears on all sides.

Add the cilantro (if using), garlic, Vegeta seasoning, and cumin, cover, and cook for 18 to 20 minutes, stirring occasionally. Add the boiling water and stir. Cover, reduce the heat to medium, and cook for 1 hour and 35 minutes, stirring occasionally as needed or until the meat is tender and the onions are jammy. Serve.

Bun Gaxwo
IIBKA IYO
SHIIDISTA
BUN KHAXWAH
Jamro

CHAPTER 8

Macmacaan *(DESSERTS)*

This beloved dessert has several names: shushumow, kalkals, and zinanaande. Its ingredients are pantry staples, and it is fried, then tossed in a simple sugar syrup. The shushumow are formed by shaping the pastry with any one of a range of tools. Either a brand new, sanitized afro pick or a gnocchi or shushumow board will allow you to make the classic elongated shushumow shape (in this recipe, I'm using an afro pick). People also use the back of a fork, a cheese grater, a colander, or whatever they might have on hand that will give the shushumow their characteristic ridged surface. Different tools make for slightly differently shaped shushumow. This crispy and sweet pastry is a perfect afternoon snack served with bitter qaxwo (coffee). Shushumow stores well for a few days, which makes it a great hostess gift to make in advance.

Shushumow *(SWEET FRIED-SHELL PASTRY)*

MAKES ABOUT 27 PIECES

For the Dough

2 cups (256 g) all-purpose flour, plus more for dusting

⅓ cup (80 ml) canola oil, plus more for frying

¼ cup (60 ml) water

1 large egg

2 tablespoons sugar

¼ teaspoon salt

For the Glaze

¼ cup (50 g) sugar

¼ cup (60 ml) water

To make the dough, combine the flour, canola oil, water, egg, sugar, and salt in a large bowl. Stir together, then knead until a dough forms, about 5 minutes.

Generously flour a clean work surface. Pinch off a marble-sized piece of dough and roll it into a ball on the floured work surface. Flatten the ball against the tines of an afro pick, patting and stretching it out to a rough oval about 2½ inches (6.5 cm) long and 1 inch (2.5 cm) wide. Grasp one of the longer edges of the dough oval and start rolling it down to form a little cylinder with ridges from the pick's tines in its surface. Set aside and repeat with the rest of the dough.

Pour 1½ inches (4 cm) of canola oil into a large, deep skillet over medium heat. Place a paper towel–lined baking sheet or plate beside the stove. Once the oil is shimmering, start adding the shushumow, stirring the oil in a circular motion so that they cook evenly. The shushumow are done when they are golden brown all around, 2 to 3 minutes. With tongs or a slotted spoon, remove the fried shushumow to the paper towel–lined plate or baking sheet.

Recipe continues

To make the glaze, combine the sugar and water in a small pot and bring to a boil. Continue to boil the mixture until it reduces to a thick syrup, 4 to 5 minutes. Turn off the heat under the syrup and add the shushumow to the pot, tossing and stirring gently to coat them evenly in the syrup. Use a large spoon to carefully transfer the shushumow to another parchment paper-lined plate; they will harden as they sit. They can be eaten right away and will keep for 7 days in an airtight container.

It is an ongoing joke that Somalis, especially elders, have a big sweet tooth. Our cuisine reflects our love for sweet things and, for us, dessert is not an afterthought. The dishes in this chapter are just a glimpse of the Somali dessert and sweets landscape. During casariyo (afternoon tea break), we serve and share sweets like doolsho (page 209), xalwo (page 212), shushumow (page 205), and buskud (page 215). Some treats, like rooti farmaajo (page 219) or moos bukeeni (page 227), are Ramadan staples. Other desserts like labaniyad (page 223) and doolsho timir (page 234) are connected to martiqaads (gatherings for special guests in one's home). The most common spice in Somali desserts is cardamom, which is to our sweets what xawaash is to our savory foods. Cinnamon and nutmeg are also commonly used, and in the diaspora, vanilla has become popular. Like savory dishes, many Somali desserts are regional specialties, and the culinary expertise of people from a dish's region of origin is highly regarded.

While *doolsho* is the Somali word for cakes generally, this airy doolsho is the most well-known Somali cake. It's not uncommon for entrepreneurial ladies to set up neighborhood cake stands, where they pack warm cakes into bright bags to be carried home and paired with shaah (spiced tea) and gleaming cuts of xalwo, crunchy shushumow (fried pastry), and freshly baked buskud (cookies) for an intoxicating casariyo (afternoon tea). Doolsho gets its intoxicating, floral scent from cardamom and often includes other spices or vanilla. It's very light and moist thanks to the whipped egg whites that are gently folded into sweetened, spiced egg yolks. It's hard to believe a cake this simple can be this good.

Doolsho *(CARDAMOM CAKE)*

SERVES 8 TO 10

Canola oil, for greasing the pan

1 cup plus 2 tablespoons (148 g) all-purpose flour, plus more for dusting

6 large eggs, separated

1 cup (200 g) sugar

1 teaspoon ground cardamom

½ teaspoon ground cinnamon (optional)

1 teaspoon baking powder

¼ teaspoon fine sea salt

Preheat the oven to 350°F (180°C). Grease a 12-cup Bundt pan with canola oil and dust lightly with flour; set aside.

In a medium bowl, beat the egg whites until stiff peaks form; set aside.

In a large mixing bowl, whisk together the sugar, egg yolks, cardamom, and cinnamon (if using). Gently fold in the egg whites until they are thoroughly combined with the yolk mixture.

In a small bowl, sift together the flour, baking powder, and salt. Add the flour mixture into the egg mixture in batches, stirring to combine. Pour the batter into the prepared Bundt pan and bake for 17 to 20 minutes, until a piece of raw spaghetti or a cake tester comes out clean. Let the cake cool in the pan, invert it onto a cake plate or stand, and serve.

DHOOL BARI COOKING SCHOOL

In Bosaso, a beautiful but swelteringly hot city located on the northeastern coast of Somalia, there is a cooking classroom buzzing with activity. Here, eager local girls learn how to make all manner of sweets, as well as traditional savory Somali dishes. Bari Cooking School was founded in 2019 by Xaawo Mohamed Issa Mohamed, a daughter of Somalia who returned to her motherland after decades spent abroad in London.

Born in 1964 in the Waberi district of Mogadishu, Xaawo had an idyllic childhood in the capital city. She spent her early years at the side of her maternal grandmother and her mother, watching them cook meals for the family over the burjiko (Somali charcoal stove). By the time she was eight, she was assisting them. She fondly recalls primary school days, when mothers dropped off hot lunches for their children and aunties set up shop outside schools to sell hot sandwiches filled with suugo (pasta sauce) or bajiye (black-eyed pea fritters) and potatoes served with a side of fiery hot sauce. By the time Xaawo was fifteen, she had assumed the responsibility for cooking for her family.

In 1987, she left Somalia to continue her studies, first in Kenya and then in India. Upon her graduation, she traveled to Italy—in part to buy supplies for the beauty parlor she dreamed of opening in Somalia. But Somalia was on the precipice of its calamitous Civil War, and her father urged her not to return but to establish a new life abroad.

By 1990, Xaawo had made her way to London with her new husband. At that time, the Somali community in London was relatively small—it was not until 1992 that Somali refugees fleeing the now-raging Somali Civil War would arrive en masse. As the community grew, Xaawo became involved with a women's center where Somali women met every Friday—she would remain there until 2006. She also became known as a go-to baker in the community. It started in 1992, when she made Somali sweets for her daughter Hafsa's first birthday and invited women and children from the neighborhood. The women, who were homesick for their prewar lives, were delighted by these treats from home. From that point on, Xaawo was the go-to person for catering events.

In 2019, after their youngest child went off to university, Xaawo and her husband relocated to Bosaso to care for her ill mother. Perpetually in tune with her community's needs, she noticed that baking supplies were in short supply—everything needed to be imported from abroad. Perceiving that local girls needed both culinary education and a space of their own, Xaawo opened a suite of businesses: Bari Cooking School, a baking supply store, Bari Exclusive Beauty Salon, and a women-only social and event space. These ventures allowed her to finally fulfill her prewar dream of owning a beauty salon in Somalia, and also to make good use of all the cooking knowledge she had acquired in her lifetime.

Today, Bari Cooking School educates girls who never learned to make Somali foods or are interested in starting a culinary business (or both). Girls take classes for three or four hours daily and come away with both hands-on experience and written recipes. These are a novelty in Somali culture, where knowledge has been passed down from mothers to daughters in a centuries-old oral tradition.

Today, Xaawo is in the process of expanding her program to Somali universities with a goal of offering a formal certification in culinary arts. Over the phone with me, she shared that her friends back in the UK wonder why she established her businesses in Somalia and not in London. She feels strongly that these services are most needed back home—and that she has a responsibility to give back to her motherland. This also feels to her like the first and best opportunity she's had to realize her dreams to their fullest extent.

Xaawo sees her work as empowerment for women and for a new generation of Somali girls. The young women who have passed through her culinary program boost their local economies when they open successful food-based business ventures. Bari Cooking School is also preserving Somali culinary traditions for the future, in a time when many Somali foodways are at serious risk of being lost, all in the space of a few generations. It is Xaawo's hope that one day some of her students will take over and carry on her businesses—because, as she says with a laugh, "Sweets make people happy."

While the origin of xalwo, or halwa, is lost in the mist of time, the first written recipe for this sticky, sweet dessert dates back to the thirteenth-century Kitab al-Tabikh, or Book of Dishes, which includes many variations of this gelatinous treat. Long before that, it had spread throughout the Middle East and swaths of Asia and Africa, evolving different variations that incorporated a range of nuts, fruits, sweeteners, and grains. The Somali version, xalwo (pronounced *halwo*), is served during casariyo (afternoon tea) or as dessert after a large meal. It is often accompanied by cookies, cakes, and steaming cups of unsweetened qaxwo (coffee).

Xalwo *(HALWA)*

SERVES 6 TO 8

2 cups (400 g) sugar

3 cups (720 ml) water

1 cup (125 g) cornstarch

⅛ teaspoon orange food coloring

⅛ teaspoon yellow food coloring

⅓ cup (90 ml) ghee

½ teaspoon ground nutmeg

½ teaspoon ground cardamom

In a medium nonstick pot, combine the sugar and 2 cups (480 ml) of the water. Set over medium-high heat and cook, stirring, until the sugar dissolves and a sugar syrup forms, about 1 minute.

In a small bowl, combine the remaining 1 cup (240 ml) of water with the cornstarch and the orange and yellow food coloring and mix well. Add this cornstarch slurry to the pot with the sugar syrup. Mix frequently for 3 to 4 minutes as the xalwo cooks and starts to thicken. Once the xalwo is really thick and gelatinous, begin mixing it continuously. Add the ghee one spoonful at a time, along with a little of the nutmeg and cardamom, and stir continuously, incorporating each addition. As the xalwo begins to get very thick, add any remaining ghee and spices, continuing to stir in a circular motion so it doesn't stick to the pan.

Continue to swirl the xalwo with a spoon and cook until the ghee separates from the xalwo and starts expelling it. At the 45-minute mark, when the xalwo has stiffed significantly but is gelatinous, transfer it to a plate and let it cool. It should be about 7½ inches (19 cm) across and 1 to 1½ inches (2.5 to 4 cm) thick. Once the xalwo has cooled to almost room temperature but is still slightly warm, cut it into pieces and serve. You can also freeze the xalwo for another time and warm it up in the microwave before serving.

These fragrant cardamom cookies are made in several shapes, the most recognizable of which are a long rectangle and a flower or clover shape. This delicious dessert, a beloved treat from many people's childhoods, is almost always on Somali tables—brought out as a sweet treat for casariyo (afternoon tea), sometimes with sticky, bright orange pieces of xalwo sandwiched between two buskud. Buskud is also a big part of Somali Eid traditions: Families nibble them and other midmorning sweets and sip coffee following Eid prayers (and before the famed Eid nap). This recipe makes plenty to gift to loved ones while keeping some for yourself. A biscuit/cookie press, such as the one made by Marcato, is the go-to piece of equipment for making buskud. Buskud can last for weeks when stored properly in an airtight container.

Buskud *(CARDAMOM COOKIES)*

MAKES ABOUT 75 COOKIES

- 3 large eggs
- ⅓ cup (80 ml) whole milk
- ¼ cup (60 ml) canola oil
- ¼ cup (60 ml) room-temperature ghee
- 4½ cups (576 g) all-purpose flour, plus more for dusting
- 1 cup plus 3 tablespoons (234 g) sugar
- 1 tablespoon baking powder
- 1 teaspoon ground cardamom
- ¼ teaspoon salt

In a large bowl, mix together the eggs, milk, canola oil, and ghee. Combine the flour, sugar, baking powder, cardamom, and salt in a separate bowl, then add them to the liquid ingredients, mix to combine, and knead until a dough forms. Let the dough sit for 15 minutes.

Preheat the oven to 350°F (180°C) and line several baking sheets with parchment paper.

Fit a biscuit press with a flower disc or a striped disc and fill it with dough, and squeeze out cookies one at a time, transferring them to the prepared baking sheets. Make sure to work in batches, and keep any extra dough chilled while you work.

Bake the cookies for 10 to 15 minutes, depending on size, until they are light brown. Let the buskud cool before serving.

Icun translates to "eat me" in Somali, and when this cookie appears, people often sing "*icun, icalaanji, caloosha iggee,*" which translates to "eat me, chew me, take me to the stomach." This pale little cookie with the red dot is a fixture in the dessert boxes given out at Somali weddings. It is also served for dessert alongside xalwo, buskud (cardamom cookies), shushumow (sweet fried pastry), and shaah (spiced tea). This recipe calls for almond flour, which makes for a crispier and nuttier cookie. If you prefer to omit the almond flour, reduce the cardamom to ¼ teaspoon, reduce the sugar slightly, and omit the olive oil.

Icun *(SHORTBREAD COOKIES)*

MAKES ABOUT 15 COOKIES

½ cup (125 g) salted butter, softened

⅓ cup (65 g) sugar

1 cup (128 g) all-purpose flour

¼ cup (28 g) almond flour

1 tablespoon olive oil, plus more as needed

1 teaspoon vanilla extract

½ teaspoon ground cardamom

Red food coloring

Using a hand mixer at medium speed, whip the softened butter in a bowl for 1 minute. Add the sugar and beat into the butter for 3 minutes, until the sugar disappears completely into the butter.

Add the all-purpose flour, almond flour, olive oil, vanilla, and cardamom at once. Mix until a smooth, firm dough forms; add a splash more olive oil if needed. Cover the dough and let it rest in the fridge for 1 hour.

Preheat the oven to 350°F (180°C) and line a baking sheet with parchment paper. Scoop up about 1 tablespoon of dough and roll it between your palms into a smooth ball. Place on the lined baking sheet and flatten very slightly so that it looks a little more disc-like. Repeat with the remaining dough, leaving enough space between the cookies for them to expand during the cooking process. Dab a very small dot of red food coloring onto the center of each cookie.

Bake the cookies for 10 to 12 minutes, or until they are a very light golden color on both top and bottom. Let the cookies cool before serving.

Rooti farmaajo translates to "cheese bread"; this sweet bread is also called honeycomb bread. It is a close cousin of Yemeni khaliat al nahl (honeycomb bread), which is unsurprising considering Somalia's proximity to Yemen. The toppings are where the cousins part ways: khaliat al nahl is topped with syrup and seeds, while rooti farmaajo is topped with sweetened condensed milk and shredded coconut flakes. Rooti farmaajo is particularly popular during Ramadan, but it can be enjoyed at any time of year, served with coffee or tea.

Rooti Farmaajo *(SWEET CHEESE BREAD)*

MAKES ABOUT 30 ROLLS

2 large eggs

⅔ cup (160 ml) warm whole milk, plus more as needed

7 teaspoons sugar

2 teaspoons active dry yeast

2¼ cups (288 g) all-purpose flour, plus more as needed

½ teaspoon ground cardamom

¼ teaspoon fine sea salt

¼ teaspoon baking powder

¼ teaspoon ground cinnamon

3 tablespoons salted butter, melted

Canola oil, for greasing

1 (8-ounce / 225 g) package cream cheese

¼ cup (60 ml) sweetened condensed milk

¼ cup (20 g) unsweetened finely shredded coconut flakes

Crack each of the 2 eggs into a separate bowl and beat both. Set aside. In a small bowl, combine the milk, sugar, and yeast and set aside for 10 minutes until foamy.

In a large bowl, combine the flour, cardamom, salt, baking powder, and cinnamon; mix. Add the yeast mixture to the dry ingredients along with the butter and 1 of the beaten eggs. Knead until a dough comes together, adding more flour as needed, then grease the surface of the dough with a little oil, cover, and set aside in a warm place for 1 hour, until doubled in size.

Preheat the oven to 350°F (180°C). Grease a 9-inch (23 cm) cake pan with oil.

Divide the dough in two and use your hands to roll one-half into a rope, then cut the rope into 15 equal pieces. Flatten each piece of dough into a disk with a rolling pin and place a bean-sized piece of cream cheese in the center. Fold the edges of the dough circle up toward the center and pinch it closed over the cream cheese. Roll it into a ball between your palms and place it in the greased pan. Repeat this process with all the dough and make sure the cheese-filled balls are evenly spaced in a single layer in the pan. Mix a splash of milk into the remaining egg. Let the dough rise in the pan for 15 minutes, then brush the tops of the balls with the egg-milk mixture. Bake until golden brown, 12 to 15 minutes.

Remove the rolls from the oven, drizzle with condensed milk to your liking while the rolls are still warm and sprinkle with shredded coconut. Serve warm.

Macsharo is yet another delicious Reer Xamar contribution to Somali cuisine—and, thanks to its use of rice and corn flours, it's also gluten free. It's a sweet snack that is often found in the dessert boxes that are given to guests at Somali weddings. Macsharo needs several hours to rise and develop its texture, so plan accordingly. (If you are short on time, a 1-hour rise will work; however, the longer rise helps with achieving its desired texture.) You can cook it on the stovetop as described below, but if that's not an option, you can bake it, covered, at 350°F (180°C) for 15 minutes. Note the rice flour for the batter should be regular rice flour, not glutinous rice flour.

Macsharo (SWEET RICE CAKE)

MAKES 3 LARGE MACSHARO; SERVES 12

For the Starter

¼ cup (60 ml) warm water

2 tablespoons white corn flour

2½ teaspoons active dry yeast

2 teaspoons sugar

For the Syrup

1¼ cups (300 ml) water

1 cup (200 g) sugar

½ teaspoon ground cardamom

For the Batter

3 cups (384 g) rice flour

¼ teaspoon baking powder

¼ teaspoon salt

¼ teaspoon ground cardamom

2 cups (480 ml) water

1 large egg

6 tablespoons of ghee, for frying

To make the starter, in a small bowl, mix together the water, white corn flour, yeast, and sugar. Set aside for 10 minutes, until the mixture is foamy.

To make the syrup, combine the water, sugar, and cardamom in a small pot. Set it over medium-high heat and cook, stirring, until the sugar dissolves and a syrup forms, 3 to 4 minutes. Set aside to cool.

To make the batter, in a large bowl, mix together the rice flour, baking powder, salt, and cardamom, then mix in the water and egg to form a batter. Stir in the starter and the cooled syrup, cover the bowl, and set aside in a warm place for 3 hours, until it has risen significantly.

Heat 2 tablespoons of ghee in a 9-inch non-stick skillet, over low heat until melted. Swirl it around the bottom and up the sides of the pan to make sure the pan is evenly greased. Pour in a third of the batter (about 2 cups / 480 ml) and swirl the batter in the pan, then allow the batter to start setting. After about 1 minute, once the batter is no longer runny, cover the skillet and cook undisturbed for 10 minutes. Check the color of the bottom of the macsharo. If it is beginning to turn dark brown or is at risk of burning, flip and cook for another 5 minutes. Otherwise, continue cooking for another 5 minutes without flipping. Remove the cover; the macsharo should look spongy and thick with crispy brown edges. Run a spatula

around the edge and under the macsharo to loosen it. Lift the macsharo, transfer it to a plate, and cover it. Repeat the cooking process twice more with the remaining batter. Once cooled, slice each macsharo into 4 wedges, for a total of 12 pieces.

Labaniyad is a popular dessert, served cool during Ramadan or paired with fresh fruits (berries, mango, melon, banana, pineapple) at special gatherings. A boxed custard mix is often used, but making the custard from scratch is easy, and the results are delicious.

Labaniyad *(CREAMY CARDAMOM CUSTARD)*

SERVES 4

6 egg yolks

¼ cup (30 g) cornstarch

5 tablespoons (75 g) sugar

1 teaspoon vanilla extract

¼ teaspoon ground cardamom

⅛ teaspoon ground nutmeg

2 cups (480 ml) whole milk

1 cup (240 ml) heavy whipping cream

In a large bowl, mix together the egg yolks, cornstarch, sugar, vanilla, cardamom, and nutmeg. Set aside.

In a large pot over medium heat, combine the milk and cream and heat until hot but not boiling. Take the pot off the stove and, 1 tablespoon at a time, whisk the cornstarch-egg mixture into the pot until it's fully incorporated. Set the pot back over medium-high heat, whisking continuously until the liquid thickens, about 6 minutes. Pour the custard into a big bowl and cover the top with plastic wrap, gently pressing the plastic onto the surface of the custard to keep it from forming a skin.

You can serve the custard as soon as it reaches room temperature or, if you wish, chill it in the fridge for 3 to 4 hours before serving.

Mashmash is an incredibly delicious, slightly greasy Somali pastry that is essentially a cardamom-flavored fried pancake. It's typically eaten at casariyo (afternoon teatime), during Ramadan, or at weddings or other special celebrations. Mashmash is very sweet and pairs well with plain qaxwo (coffee).

Mashmash *(SWEET FRIED PANCAKE)*

MAKES 12 PANCAKES

1¾ cups (420 ml) water

1 cup (200 g) sugar

2 cups (256 g) all-purpose flour

¼ teaspoon ground cardamom

¼ teaspoon salt

1 cup (240 ml) vegetable or canola oil

In a small pot over high heat, combine ½ cup (120 ml) of the water and the sugar and boil, stirring, until the sugar melts down into a syrup, about 5 minutes.

In a large mixing bowl, combine the flour, cardamom, salt, the remaining 1½ cups (300 ml) of water, and the warm sugar syrup. Stir together until a batter forms.

Set a plate lined with a thick layer of paper towels next to the stove. In a small, deep skillet, heat the oil over medium-high heat until it's shimmering. Pour in ¼ cup (60 ml) of batter and cook for 40 seconds on one side, then turn and cook for 20 seconds on the second side, until both sides of the pancake are firm and no longer runny. Spoon oil over the center of the pancake to help it fry evenly.

Transfer the pancake to the paper towel-lined plate and repeat the process, replenishing oil as needed, until all the batter is gone and there is a small stack of fried mashmash. Blot excess oil off the mashmash and let them cool completely before serving.

This popular Ramadan dessert is a regional dish; plantains are not eaten in all parts of Somalia. In the south, where they are a staple, agricultural workers cook firm green plantains savory-style in suugo (tomato sauce) as a meat replacement. For moos bukeeni, ripe plantains are cooked in sugar syrup until they are tender and caramelized; added cardamom and ghee give the plantains a rich flavor. Make sure to select ripe plantains with skin that is streaked black; these are the sweetest. Enjoy with unsweetened qaxwo (coffee).

Moos Bukeeni *(CARAMELIZED PLANTAINS)*

SERVES 3 OR 4

¼ cup (50 g) sugar

3 large ripe plantains, peeled and sliced diagonally

3 cups (720 ml) water

2 tablespoons ghee

½ teaspoon ground cardamom

In a nonstick pot over medium-high heat, heat the sugar without stirring until it is melted and slightly brown, 1 to 2 minutes.

Add the sliced plantains and stir to coat them in the sugar. Carefully add the water, ghee, and cardamom and gently stir once to incorporate. Cook covered over low heat for 25 to 30 minutes, stirring occasionally to prevent sticking, until the liquid is reduced to a syrupy consistency and the plantains are caramelized. Remove from the heat and serve warm.

MUHSEN HIRABE, BANANA FARMER

In the lush and fertile farming lands of Janaale in southern Somalia, thirty-five-year-old Muhsen Hirabe owns the largest banana farm in the country. Established by Muhsen's politician-turned-farmer father, this stunning 250-hectare farm, called Buurta Sheekh Abukar Hirabe, has been in the family for more than forty years, predating the Somali Civil War.

Though he was born in Mogadishu in 1990, Muhsen comes from a large extended family of farmers from the Lower Shabelle region. Muhsen grew up doing chores around the family farm, then spent several years studying abroad in Indonesia and Thailand before relocating to Wisconsin for five years. In 2020, he returned to Somalia, finally ready to take over the family farm.

On the farm, the main crop is the creamy—and famous—Somali banana. (It's difficult to imagine modern Somali cuisine without the humble banana. This fruit is both a staple of Somali cuisine and a reminder of the country's colonial connection to Italy.) The family also grows plantains, mangoes, grapefruit, lime, spondias, and coconuts. They employ roughly 150 workers, who commute to the farm from nearby towns; this arrangement is in contrast to the brutal sharecropping system that once existed on the Italian-owned farms in the region. While Muhsen's family farm was never owned by the colonists, relics of the colonial past and of the decades-long Somali Civil War are on view in the crumbling infrastructure of many Janaale farmlands.

Muhsen's family have weathered much, including bearing witness to the infamous Somali Banana Wars of the 1990s, when rival warlords wrestled for control over Somalia's $96 million banana industry. While many farmers deserted their farms to escape the violence of the war, Muhsen's stayed and, in time, they also managed to thrive.

When Muhsen returned to the farm, he faced many obstacles. Much of the modern equipment he needed was not available in the country, and he quickly decided to be his own supplier, starting a business importing farming supplies and equipment. He had containers full of equipment and other materials delivered to Mogadishu's port. Within two years, his reputation for importing high-quality and unique products led other farmers to begin purchasing from him.

As soon as Muhsen figured out his supply issues, he began to face a new set of problems: taxation from both the government and the fundamentalist group al-Shabaab, which holds power in the farming regions of southern Somalia. In order for Muhsen's bananas to make it to market, they have to pass through at least twelve separate paid checkpoints (called *isbaaro*) between Janaale and the markets in Mogadishu and other cities. Some are run by the government and some by al-Shabaab: All exact money before allowing goods to pass. Muhsen estimates that by the time his bananas make it to Gaalkacyo, Hargeisa, Burco, or Mogadishu, he's already lost 40 percent of any potential profit to checkpoint fees.

According to Muhsen, al-Shabaab is not at the root of his issue. Rather, he points to the weakness of a Somali government that offers him no protections from al-Shabaab nor any subsidies as a farmer—and yet taxes him at multiple checkpoints. He states that if the government was strong enough to do its job, farmers like him would not have to raise prices just to break even. The result is that the average Somali consumer, who lives in a country where the per capita GDP is $590 a year, cannot afford Somali-grown bananas or other foods grown in their own country. As a result, small scale farms are failing, with families who come from generations of farmers losing their homes and turning into internally displaced people (IDPs) in makeshift camps. In fact, according to the Internal Displacement Monitoring Centre, as of 2023, 3.9 million Somalis are internally displaced. This issue is close to Muhsen; he can count at least one hundred people he knows who are displaced from farms in Janaale, among them his own uncle.

In addition to the lack of government support and viable market options, farmers also flee their homes to escape the violence of groups like al-Shabaab. Muhsen relates that in a region known for cambuulo (a traditional adzuki bean dish), the indigenous bean is now imported because no one remains on the land to grow it, and the knowledge of how to do so is being lost.

Muhsen sees how these factors have a larger impact on Somali foodways. With the rise of imports in Somali society and the waning of Somali farmers, indigenous Somali food is increasingly seen as lower-class food, while imported food is a marker of higher status. The indigenous dishes that were staples in rural and farming areas are being abandoned in favor of imported foods. As a farmer, Muhsen worries that the idea of what Somali food truly is will slowly disappear.

He knows that his farm, while never far from needing to shut down, has been able to survive largely due to support from his family's real estate investments in Mogadishu. Other small-scale farmers are not so fortunate. Muhsen is vocal about these issues on social media. He has tried his hand at organizing fellow farmworkers to demand more from the government. He believes that if farmers shut down production in protest, the larger society would be forced to listen. But there are limits on how vocal he feels he can be. Speaking out can mean risking his own life, with potential threat coming from various actors, including the Somali government, US forces, al-Shabaab, and private mercenaries. These fears are not unfounded; there has been a recent uptick in the slaying of Somali farmers. Notably, in 2024, a highly educated Somali-Swedish farmer named Amun Abdullahi was brutally gunned down on her own farm by a group of masked men.

Despite all these challenges, Muhsen is determined to save his family farm, and to do so by keeping it profitable via creative ventures. He plans to start a sheep farm, supplying meat to restaurants and offering meat-delivery subscriptions to private homes. With the sheep, he can also avoid the isbaaro, or checkpoint system, since the herds are not taxed at checkpoint, which would allow him to turn a profit without having to charge his customers so much.

As for what could help Somali farmers, Muhsen is clear: A strong centralized government could both protect farmers from the isbaaro system and also offer them subsidies and other support for growing food locally. A functioning government could fund large-scale soil testing, allowing farmers to know about and work to improve the health of their soil. With these support systems—enjoyed by growers in many other countries—farmers like Muhsen could continue to do the critical work of cutting Somali dependency on imports and foreign aid while also growing food for their fellow citizens and preserving indigenous Somali foodways.

The origins of this sweet caramel-like dessert are in its name: Hailing from Brava, Somalia, it also is known as peera by some, which might show its connections to the Indian dessert of the same name. This milk fudge needs simple ingredients and time. It requires minimal work, just the occasional stir over the course of an hour and a half as the heat does its magic. Roll the fudge into balls while it's still warm and enjoy it as a sweet treat during casariyo (afternoon tea) or gift it to loved ones on special occasions like Eid.

Caano Baraawe *(CARAMEL MILK FUDGE)*

MAKES ABOUT 26 PIECES

2 cups (480 ml) whole milk

1 cup plus 2 tablespoons (225 g) sugar

¼ teaspoon ground cardamom

4 tablespoons buttermilk

3 tablespoons flour

Melted ghee, to shape

In a small nonstick pot over medium-high heat, combine the milk and sugar and bring to a simmer. Adjust the heat to low and cook down over a low simmer, stirring occasionally so it does not burn. After an hour, stir in the cardamom, buttermilk, and flour and, stirring as needed, cook until the caano baraawe is thick and the fudge has turned into an earthy brown, about 30 more minutes.

Pour and scrape the fudge from the pot onto a plate greased lightly with ghee or another flat surface. Once the fudge has cooled down but is still warm, rub a little ghee onto your hands and roll the fudge into small round balls. Serve warm or at room temperature, or store in an airtight container in the fridge for several days.

While doolsho timir is not as widely known as the classic cardamom doolsho (page 209), it is just as delicious. This cake, which was documented in the 1970s in *A Cookery of Somali Style* (one of the earliest Somali cookbooks), fell out of favor for a time. However, it is now experiencing a resurgence, particularly in Somali restaurants in the diaspora. This doolsho gets the majority of its sweetness from the ripe, sticky Medjool dates that are at its core. The buttermilk glaze is optional, but its tang offers a nice contrast to the sweet caramel flavor of the dates. If you prefer a heavier glaze, double the glaze recipe. This is a perfect cake for casariyo, the afternoon tea meal. Serve with cups of bitter qaxwo (coffee) or enjoy it on its own.

Doolsho Timir *(DATE CAKE)*

MAKES ONE 9-INCH (23 CM) ROUND CAKE

For the Cake

⅓ cup plus 1 tablespoon (95 ml) canola oil, plus more for greasing the pan

1 cup (240 ml) milk, heated to a near boil

12 large pitted Medjool dates

4 large eggs

¼ cup (45 g) packed brown sugar

1 cup (128 g) all-purpose flour

1 teaspoon baking powder

½ teaspoon fine sea salt

½ teaspoon baking soda

½ teaspoon ground cardamom

For the Glaze

¼ cup (30 g) powdered sugar

2 tablespoons buttermilk

1 tablespoon salted butter, melted

⅛ teaspoon ground cardamom

Preheat the oven to 350°F (180°C). Grease a 9-inch (23 cm) round cake or Bundt pan and set aside.

To make the cake, in a small bowl, pour the hot milk over the dates, cover with a metal lid and let soak for 10 minutes.

In a large bowl, mix the eggs, canola oil, and brown sugar.

In a small bowl, sift together the flour, baking powder, salt, baking soda, and cardamom. Add these dry ingredients to the egg mixture; stir together. Mash the soaked dates and milk together into a thickened paste, or blend until smooth, and stir into the batter.

Pour the batter into the prepared cake pan, place in the oven, and bake for 20 to 25 minutes or until a piece of uncooked spaghetti or a cake tester comes out clean. Set aside to cool.

Meanwhile, make the glaze. In a small bowl, mix together the powdered sugar, buttermilk, melted butter, and cardamom. Set aside while the cake cools.

Transfer the cake to a plate or cake stand and drizzle with the glaze, using as much as you'd like.

CHAPTER 9

Cabitaan *(DRINKS)*

Shaah is one of the most beloved of all Somali drinks, and everyone has their particular way to make and serve it. When served without milk, it's called shaah bigays or shaah rinji; served with milk (either fresh or powdered), it's called shaah cadays. It's spiced with cardamom, cloves, ginger, cinnamon, and sometimes nutmeg. Shaah is similar to Yemeni, Kenyan, and Indian chais, one difference being that, in shaah, the milk is added at the end; another being that there is no black pepper in Somali tea. It's not particularly thick, but it's almost always very sweet. Usually a family will make one or two large kettles of shaah to drink from throughout the day—especially at casariyo, the afternoon tea meal. Serve, if you like, with the milk of your choice—possibly the Somali favorite, Nido brand powdered milk.

Shaah *(SPICED SOMALI TEA)*

SERVES 12

3 quarts (2.8 L) water

2 (3- to 4-inch / 7.5 to 10 cm) cinnamon sticks

4 whole cloves

7 whole green cardamom pods

1 (3-ounce / 84 g) piece unpeeled fresh ginger

⅔ to ¾ cup (135 to 150 g) sugar, to taste

4 teaspoons loose-leaf black tea, or 2 or 3 tea bags

Milk, for serving (optional)

Bring the water to boil in a large pot over medium-high heat. In a mortar and pestle, pound the cinnamon, cloves, and cardamom pods into small pieces; add these to the water. Smash the ginger in the mortar and pestle and add it to the water. Finally, add the sugar and the tea to the water and boil for about 5 minutes. Take the tea off the burner and let it steep until it's as strong as you like it. Strain through a fine-mesh sieve and serve, with or without milk.

AYEEYO'S BLENDS

There's a Somali saying that roughly translates to "God, never take us to a house where they don't brew tea." Such is the importance of tea, or shaah, to the Somali people. Shaah's centrality to Somali identity is something that Hamda Issa-Salwe had in mind when she founded Ayeeyo's Blends, a Somali tea company, in 2020. The name honors her grandmother—her ayeeyo.

Born and raised in London, Hamda has fond memories of the warming spices her ayeeyo and mother blended for tea—always a reminder of their beloved homeland. Hamda began making her tea blends during the 2020 Covid-19 lockdown, when she found herself cooped up in her London flat, thousands of miles away from her parents (who had moved back to Somalia for their retirement). Desperately missing her family, she began cooking up traditional Somali recipes, chatting with her mother and grandmother on WhatsApp for recipe guidance and much-needed conversation. Through these daily calls, Hamda found solace in the kitchen, perfecting her execution of traditional dishes like oodkac and muufo and staying close to her loved ones despite the distance.

One day, Hamda ran out of the industrial-sized container of tea spices that her mother had blended using bulk spices from Indian shops in Southall. With her mother so far away, Hamda began mixing her own tea blend, every cup making it easier for her to navigate the isolation the pandemic brought.

As her experiments continued, she began leaving takeout containers of food and tea outside her kitchen window for her friends. Word of her delicious tea began spreading, and soon friends of friends were asking—and even offering to pay—for tea of their own. She began giving out jars full of her aromatic tea spice mix, and the buzz only grew from there.

Entrepreneurship runs in the Issa-Salwe family. Hamda's mother, Xaawo, (see page 210) runs a cooking school in Somalia; her sister runs a health and skin-care clinic in London; and back in the 1960s her ayeeyo owned a bistro connected to Mogadishu's largest cinema. It's no wonder that Xaawo encouraged her to take Ayeeyo's Blends seriously. In short order, Hamda had designed a logo, made an Instagram account, and launched her business. In 2021, Hamda's beloved ayeeyo passed away, and she began focusing on Ayeeyo's Blends full-time as a way to honor her grandmother's legacy.

The new company found success almost immediately, thanks to Hamda's keen eye for brand marketing and the word-of-mouth promotion from friends and family. She recognizes Ayeeyo's Blends' core customers—second- or third-generation Somalis of the diaspora who yearn for their culture and for the flavors they grew up with, but have neither the time nor the know-how to make tea spice blends from scratch—and often don't have access to the right ingredients. Ayeeyo's Blends is among the brands that have stepped up to fill the gaps in the market.

These days, Hamda blends and packages the aromatic spices in a commercial kitchen she leases in London. She's working toward her MBA so she has the skills she needs to help her business succeed. Her hope is that customers, Somali and non-Somali alike, come to understand and appreciate the richness of Somali tea culture. She also wants Somalis in the diaspora to be able to find their cultural foods on grocery shelves and to carry their homeland's tea practices forward, wherever they may find themselves.

Vimto (much like the similar shani) is a mixed-fruit drink that was created in England in 1908 and has become popular throughout the Muslim world—particularly during Ramadan. In the Middle East, 35 million bottles are sold each year. There may be as many ways of drinking and serving Vimto as there are households. This cordial is a straightforward combination of Vimto concentrate, water, and lime juice. Many Somalis also combine Vimto and milk. Vimto is on the sweeter side, so add more water to taste or use extra ice for a cold and refreshing drink.

Fiimto *(VIMTO FRUIT CORDIAL)*

MAKES ABOUT 7½ CUPS (1.8 L)

6 cups (1.4 L) cold water

1½ cups (360 ml) Vimto concentrate

Juice of 1 lime

Ice, for serving

In a pitcher, combine the water, Vimto concentrate, and lime juice and mix. Store in the refrigerator and serve over ice.

The Horn of Africa is the birthplace of coffee, and, understandably, this part of the world has a strong coffee culture. Somali qaxwo (pronounced *qah-wo*) is ground coffee blended with aromatic spices like ginger, cinnamon, and sometimes cardamom. The ancient Greeks called Somalia Regio Cinnamafore (the Land of Cinnamon), and the cinnamon in Somali qaxwo is a revelation, as is the warmth of the ginger. Another drink, xanshar, is made from the dried and roasted outer shell of the coffee bean.

Qaxwo is lovely at any point in the day, but it really shines in the afternoon, when many Somalis observe casariyo, the afternoon meal break. During casariyo, cups of steaming bitter and spicy qaxwo are paired with thick cuts of sweet doolsho (page 209), cookies, dates, and sticky bright-orange xalwo (page 212). You can make Somali spiced coffee as directed here, or you can buy it from a Somali grocer; brands like Banadir One have the spices already blended in.

Qaxwo *(SPICED COFFEE)*

MAKES ABOUT 4 CUPS (960 ML)

4 cups (960 ml) water

7 tablespoons (48 g) ground coffee (a light roast)

1 teaspoon ground cinnamon

¼ teaspoon ground ginger

½ teaspoon ground cardamom

Sugar, for serving

Milk, for serving

Heat the water in a pot over medium-high heat until hot; add the coffee, cinnamon, ginger, and cardamom and bring it to a rolling boil. Watch it closely—anytime it looks like it will boil over, lift it off the burner until it settles down, then put it back on the burner. Repeat two more times, for about 1 or 2 minutes. Strain and serve with sugar and milk as you like, or drink black.

BEYDAN COFFEE

Amal Dirie was born and raised in Ottawa, Canada, where her mother ran a successful café called Hanna Sweets. Amal remembers how her mother would talk of her desire to open a café in her homeland; and when Amal moved to Somalia in September 2017 to study medicine, she noticed that there was a lack of cafés in the capital. Mogadishu had once been home to numerous cafés, such as the famous 1980s hot spot Caffè Nazionale Bar, which offered cappuccinos and conversation. This rich café culture had totally disintegrated during the Civil War and had never quite rebounded.

Feeling inspired by her mother's recollections but reluctant to open a brick-and-mortar location, Amal began baking sweets from home and, with her friend Najiib Abdullahi Mohamud, she began selling them to friends and acquaintances. Soon, Amal's mother, who had also relocated to Mogadishu, was importing supplies from Kuwait to help support her daughter's endeavors. Social media and new delivery services like Gulivery boosted their business, and they began making custom cakes. Demand was high, and they added brownies, cookies, and cheesecakes to their product mix. At Najiib's urging, Amal began offering coffee as well, and the two of them began looking for a location to open a café.

When they finally found and secured a location, Amal (wanting a traditional yet unique Somali name) called their shop Beydan. The name means "almond"—a fitting title for the first Somali coffee shop to offer plant-based milk.

It was important to Amal and Najiib that Beydan be an example of modern Somali café culture and also be rooted in tradition. Their initial interior design was industrial, a direction that inspired the look of other coffee shops that opened following Beydan's success. In time, Beydan's look shifted to a Japanese/Scandinavian style—something new to Mogadishu. Along with modernity, tradition was still at the heart of Beydan, whose logo features the ancient Indigenous Alindi fabric.

Beydan opened in the Taleex neighborhood of Mogadishu in July of 2019, with four baristas and three bakers, its owners having overcome challenges ranging from construction issues and installation mishaps to being forced to import many materials from abroad. Amal and Najiib's experience with their baking business—and Najiib's careful study of Turkish cafés during his time abroad—made Beydan an immediate success; a place to see and be seen.

Over five years later, having successfully navigated the storm that was the global Covid-19 pandemic, Amal and Najiib are now married with children. And Beydan, which is sometimes referred to as the "Starbucks of Somalia," has five locations, with another planned. They import beans from neighboring Ethiopia and Kenya, have their own coffee-roasting facility, and bake their own pastries. (Somalia's own coffee production, small in scale and centered around the Cal Madow mountain range in northern Somalia, halted during the Civil War and has yet to rebound.) They are so successful that even the president of Somalia drinks Beydan's coffee. They have plans to open in the cities of Garowe and Hargeisa and in neighboring Kenya.

Today there are many Somali cafés up and running; they have Beydan to thank for single-handedly reviving Somali café culture. Beydan has stimulated the local economy, creating jobs for many young Somalis, primarily women, and giving them work training and experience. In Somali society, men traditionally go to restaurants to drink coffee and discuss politics (a tongue-in-cheek activity called *fadhi ku dirir,* or "fighting while seated") while women gather over coffee at home. Beydan has made coffee culture more youth-oriented and helped bring women into a public coffee domain. At Beydan, coffee is for everyone.

Pineapple juice is one of the most popular juices in Somalia, so much so that in the diaspora, households without access to the fruit itself will substitute powdered pineapple juice mix. If the pineapple is very sweet, you'll be able to skip the sugar. Chill the juice before serving or serve it over ice.

Biyo Cananaas *(PINEAPPLE JUICE)*

MAKES ABOUT 3 CUPS (720 ML)

1 ripe pineapple (about 4 pounds / 1.8 kg)

2 cups (480 ml) water

2 tablespoons sugar, plus more as needed (optional)

Lime wedges, for serving (optional)

Cut the top and bottom of the pineapple off with a sharp knife, then stand it up and trim the skin off of the sides. Remove any additional bumpy pineapple skin, then cut into slices. Combine the pineapple and water in a blender and blend until smooth; taste and blend in sugar as needed. Strain through a fine-mesh sieve if you'd like a smoother juice. Serve as is or over ice, with lime wedges if you like.

Mango was my favorite juice when I was growing up, and it remains my favorite to this day. It was always served at family parties. When I visited Mogadishu as an adult, the mango juice was the best I've ever had—fresh mangoes are in abundant supply in Somalia. This juice is incredibly popular (and not just with me); it's always on the menu in Somali restaurants, and you're just as likely to find it in homes. For this juice, pick the ripest, most juicy mangoes you can find, ideally Kesar, Alphonso, or Ataulfo varieties. The sweeter the mangoes, the less sugar you'll need to add.

Biyo Cambe *(MANGO JUICE)*

MAKES ABOUT 3 CUPS (720 ML)

3 medium-to-large ripe mangoes (about 3 pounds / 1.4 kg total)

1½ cups (360 ml) water

1 to 2 tablespoons sugar (optional)

Ice, for serving (optional)

Peel the mangoes and cut the flesh away from the pit. Combine the mango flesh in a blender with the water and purée; taste and add sugar as needed, blending to mix it into the juice. If the juice is too thick for your liking, feel free to thin it out with additional water. Serve with or without ice.

There are two ways to make this juice. Typically limes are squeezed by hand and their juice is mixed with water and sugar—a process familiar to those who have made fresh limeade. The second approach makes use of the entire lime, blending it whole with the other ingredients to save time. If you make it according to this method, serve it the same day you make it to avoid a bitterness that develops if the lime juice is stored.

Biyo Liimo *(LIME JUICE)*

MAKES 9 CUPS (2.1 L)

8 cups (1.9 L) water

1½ cups (300 g) sugar

6 limes, skin on, rinsed, chopped very small and de-seeded

2 cups (46 g) ice

In a blender, combine 3⅓ cups (780 ml) of the water with the sugar, limes, and ice; purée until smooth with small specks of lime rind. Strain the lime purée into a pitcher or pour directly in, depending on your preference, and stir in the remaining water. Serve immediately over ice or refrigerate until ready to serve (the same day).

Watermelon, or qare, grows well in the warm climate of Somalia, and it's both eaten for dessert and blended into a refreshing juice. If your watermelon is sweet enough on its own, omit the optional sugar. Due to watermelon's high water content, it is not necessary to add water.

Biyo Qare *(WATERMELON JUICE)*

MAKES 5 CUPS (1.2 KG)

1 small seedless watermelon (about 4 pounds / 1.8 kg)

Juice of ½ small lime

2 teaspoons sugar (optional)

Ice, for serving (optional)

Cut the rind from the watermelon and cut the flesh into chunks (make sure to remove the rind from the flesh completely as it affects the flavor). Place the flesh in a blender with the lime juice and purée until smooth; taste and blend in sugar as needed. Strain through a fine-mesh sieve if you like a smoother juice and serve as is or over ice.

There are more Somali drinks than is possible to include in this book. Some of the most popular are in this chapter, including shaah (page 239), qaxwo (page 245), and various fresh fruit juices. Camel's milk is iconic—and harder to come by (though brothers Ahmed and Abdiasis Ali of Juba Farms are working to make it more available; see page 196). Other indelible Somali drinks include the following:

cabitaan sisin (sesame milk that is sometimes sweetened; popular during Ramadan)

bambeelmo (grapefruit juice)

barax (milk, water, ice, and sometimes sugar)

caano iyo timir (milk with dates; also popular during Ramadan)

goat's milk

seytuun (guava juice)

cambe lassi (mango smoothie)

caano fiimto (Vimto milk)

cabitaan raqay (tamarind drink)

afakhaado (avocado milk)

xanshar (spiced coffee-husk drink)

isbarmuuto (lemonade)

furulaato (tropical fruit and custard drink)

isbandhees (sour apple juice)

عيد مبارك أهلاوسهلا

مرحبا بكم

REFERENCES

Abdi Latif Dahir, "Camel Milk Could Be The Next Superfood–Thanks to East Africa," *Quartz*, updated July 20, 2022, https://qz.com.

Abdulqawi A. Yusuf, "The Anglo-Abyssinian Treaty of 1897 and the Somali-Ethiopian Dispute," *Horn of Africa* 3, no. 1 (1980): 38–42.

Abdurahman Abdullahi Baadiyow, *Making Sense of Somali History* (Adonis & Abbey Publishers, 2017).

Ahmed Dualeh Jama, *The Origins and Development of Mogadishu AD 1000 to 1850* (Department of Archaeology, Uppsala University, 1996).

Ahmed Ibrahim Awale, *The Cost of the Dervish War in British Somaliland on Environment and Non-Combatants 1899–1920*, Bildhaan 21 (2021), https://digitalcommons.macalester.edu.

Ali Jimale Ahmed, *The Invention of Somalia* (Red Sea Press, 1995).

Andrew Carlson, "Pirates of Puntland, Somalia," *Origins: Current Events in Historical Perspectives*, June 2009, https://origins.osu.edu.

Andy McEwen et al., "Dietary Beliefs and Behaviour of a UK Somali Population," Journal of Human Nutrition and Dietetics 22, no. 2 (2009): 116–21, http://dx.doi.org/10.1111/j.1365-277X.2008.00939.x.

Anita Sylvia Adam, *Benadiri People of Somalia: With Particular Reference to the Reer Hamar of Mogadishu* (University of London, School of Oriental and African Studies, 2011).

Annalisa Urbano, "A 'Grandiose Future for Italian Somalia': Colonial Development Discourse, Agricultural Planning, and Forced Labor (1900–1940)," *International Labor and Working-Class History*, no. 92 (2017): 69–88, https://www.jstor.org/stable/26857462.

Anyona Ondigi, "The Languages of Food and Imagined Communities at a Somali Restaurant in Bellville, South Africa," *Matatu* 54 no. 1 (2023): 87–106, http://dx.doi.org/10.1163/18757421-05401006.

Aurora Almendral, "'If The Camel Is Fine, Our Life is Fine.' But Somali Camel Herding is in Jeopardy," *National Geographic*, May 19, 2021, https://www.nationalgeographic.com.

Britannica, "History of Somalia," by Ioan M. Lewis, https://britannica.com.

Charles H. Treakle, *The Agricultural Economy of Somalia* (US Department of Agriculture, 1989).

Chris Milton, "Somalia Used as Toxic Dumping Ground," *The Ecologist*, March 1, 2009, https://theecologist.org.

Christian Webersik, "Fighting For the Plenty: The Banana Trade in Southern Somalia," *Oxford Development Studies* 33, no. 1 (2003): 81–97, https://www.researchgate.net.

Clans in Somalia (Austrian Centre for Country of Origin and Asylum Research and Documentation, 2009), https://www.refworld.org.

Climate Fact Sheet: Somalia (Red Cross Red Crescent Climate Centre, 2021).

David M. Goldenberg, "Geographia Rabbinica: The Toponym Barbaria," *Journal of Jewish Studies* 50, no. 1 (1999): 53–73, http://dx.doi.org/10.18647/2166/JJS-1999.

Diana Garvin, "Fruit of Fascist Empire: Bananas and Italian Somaliland," *The Italianist* 43, no. 3 (2023): 439–467, https://doi.org/10.1080/02614340.2023.2257943.

Elizabeth Schmidt, "The US Helped Destroy Modern Somalia," *Jacobin*, November 21, 2022, https://jacobin.com.

"Establishment Hit by Fresh Accusations in Toxic Waste Scandal," *The Herald*, September 19, 2009, https://heraldscotland.com.

Eyder Peralta, "A First: John Kerry Makes Unannounced Visit To Somalia," *NPR*, May 5, 2015, https://www.npr.org.

Fabio Parasecoli, "How Countries Use Food to Win Friends and Influence People," *Foreign Policy*, August 20, 2022, https://foreignpolicy.com.

Fahda Kulmiye, "Historical Influences of Somali Diaspora Food Choices," essay for the University of Toronto, https://academia.edu.

Harriet Marsden, "The Growing Thirst for Camel Milk," *The Week UK*, April 16, 2024, https://theweek.com.

Helen Chapin Metz, *Somalia: A Country Study* (Library of Congress, 1993).

I. M. Lewis and Said S. Samatar, *A Pastoral Democracy: A Study of Pastoralism and Politics Among the Northern Somali of the Horn of Africa* (James Currey Publishers, 1999).

Ian Cole and David Robinson, *Somali Housing Experiences in England* (Sheffield Hallam University Centre for Regional Economic and Social Research, 2003), https://researchgate.net.

Ibrahim Ali, *Origin and History of the Somali People: Vol 1* (Punite Books, 1993).

Iman Mohamed, "Defining Soomaalinimo: Race, Labor, and Nation in Somalia Italiana" (doctoral dissertation, Harvard University, 2024), http://dash.harvard.edu.

Isma Yusuf et al., "There's No Place Like [Your] Home: Exploring Somali Hospitality As A Care-full Choreography Enhancing Somali Canadian Diasporic Wellbeing," *Wellbeing, Space and Society* 4, no. 1 (2023), https://doi.org/10.1016/j.wss.2023.100145.

Isma'il Kushkush, "After Barren Years in Somalia, Signs of Growth by the Bunch," *The New York Times*, December 13, 2014, https://www.nytimes.com.

Ismail Einashe and Matt Kennard, "In the Valley of Death: Somaliland's Forgotten Genocide," *The Nation*, October 22, 2018, https://www.thenation.com.

Jamal Gabobe, "European Travel Writing on Somaliland: The Rhetoric of Empire and the Emergence of the Somali Subject," *Bildhaan: An International Journal of Somali Studies* 19 (2019): 83–100, https://digitalcommons.macalester.edu.

Jatin Dua, "From Pirate Ports to Special Economic Zones: Violence, Regulation and Port-Making in the Somali Peninsula," DIIS working paper 2017:12, Govsea Paper Series (Danish Institute for International Studies, 2017), https://econstor.eu.

Jennifer Ott, "Somali Community in Seattle," *HistoryLink*, November 19, 2010, https://historylink.org.

Jenny Aronsen Torp et al., "Somali Women's Experiences of Cooking and Meals after Migration to Sweden," *Journal of Occupational Science* 20, no. 2 (2013), https://researchgate.net.

K. Reva Levinson, "Paul Manafort Never Believed The Rules Applied To Him; I Know—I Worked With Him for a Decade," *The Hill*, August 20, 2018, https://thehill.com.

Kamil Peter Kozlowski, "Toward Resolving the Problem of Modern Piracy; A Case Study of Somalia" (master's thesis, CUNY, 2012), https://academicworks.cuny.edu.

Lee V. Cassanelli, "The End of Slavery and the 'Problem' of Farm Labor in Colonial Somalia," *Proceedings of the Third International Congress of Somali Studies* (Il Pensiero Scientifico,1988).

Lee V. Cassanelli, *The Shaping of Somali Society: Reconstructing the History of a Pastoral People, 1600–1900* (University of Pennsylvania Press, 2016).

Maxamed Cabdi Gaandi, "Isirka Soomaalida," lecture, August 22, 2014, posted August 24, 2014 by Somali Channel TV, YouTube.com, 58 minutes.

Mohamed Abdulkadir Ali, "The Backstory of Somali Pirates Does Not Fit Neatly On The Big Screen," *HuffPost*, November 25, 2013, updated January 25, 2014, https://huffpost.com.

Mohamed Ali Hussein, "Traditional Practices of

Camel Husbandry and Management in Somalia," *Camel Forum*, no. 7 (Somali Academy of Sciences and Arts, 1987), 37–48.

Mohamed Haji Mukhtar, *Historical Dictionary of Somalia*, rev. ed., Historical Dictionaries of Africa (Scarecrow Press, 2003).

Mohamed Nuuh Ali, "A Linguistic Outline of Early Somali History," *Ufahamu: A Journal of African Studies* 12, no. 3 (1983): https://doi.org/10.5070/F7123017147.

Muhammad M. Mohammadain, "Somalia in Ibn Battuta's Travel Account 'Tuhfat Al-Nuzzar,'" *Proceedings of the Second International Congress of Somali Studies* 2 (1984).

Neville Chittick, "Mediaeval Mogadishu," *Paideuma: Mitteilungen zur Kulturkunde* 28 (1982): 45–62. https://www.jstor.org/stable/41409873.

No Redress: Somalia's Forgotten Minorities (Minority Rights Group International, 2010), https://minorityrights.org.

Nuredin Hagi Scikei, *Exploring the Old Stone Town of Mogadishu* (Cambridge Scholars Publishing, 2017).

Omar Faruk, "Ethiopia and a Breakaway Somali Region Sign a Deal Giving Ethiopia Access To The Sea, Leaders Say," Associated Press, January 1, 2024, https://apnews.com.

Oxford Bibliographies, "Somalia," by Mohamed Diriye Abdullahi, last updated May 24, 2017, https://oxfordbibliographies.com.

Oxford Research Encyclopedias, "Long Distance Trade in Somalia, 1st–19th Centuries AD," by Alfredo Gonzalez Ruibal, January 31, 2023, https://oxfordre.com

Paige Roberts, *Securing Somali Fisheries* (One Earth Future Foundation, 2015), https://doi.org/10.18289/OEF.2015.001.

Paleolithic City of Jaleelo (Horn Heritage Foundation, 2023).

"'Pirate Trails' Tracks Dirty Money Resulting From Piracy Off the Horn of Africa," press release (World Bank Group, 2013), https://worldbank.org.

Potentially Important Food Plants of Somalia (Food Plant Solutions Field Guide – Somalia, Version 3, January 2022), https://foodplantsolutions.org.

Rajiv Golla, "The Secret History of Somali Breakfasts in Harlem," *Roads & Kingdoms*, December 10, 2015, https://roadsandkingdoms.com.

Ralphael Chijioke Njoku, *The History of Somalia* (Greenwood, 2013).

Report on Somaliland (Four Power Commission for Investigation for the Former Italian Colonies, Appendices to Volume II, 1948).

Said M. Shidad Hussein, "Social and Economic Developments in Pre-Islamic Somalia: Introducing African-Arabian-Mediterranean Interaction," *Antiquity—Including the "East" as "Western Identity,"* May 2023, https://researchgate.net.

Similola Coker, *The Somali Sailors*, Ethnic Communities Oral History Project (Hammersmith United Charities), https://hamunitedcharities.org.uk.

Somali Bantu History (Somali Bantu Community Association), https://somalibantumaine.org.

Somalia (US Department of State, 2011).

Somalia Political Intelligence Report, no. 2, May 24, 1947, FO 1015/140 (held at the National Archives in Britain).

Somalia: Language and Culture (New York University, 2012).

"The Hard Life of a Somali Shepherd," *The Economist*, June 10, 2017, https://theeconomist.com.

"Tsunami Exposes Somalia Toxic Waste," *Al Jazeera*, March 4, 2005, https://aljazeera.com.

BANAADIR MALL
BANAADIR MALL

GLOSSARY

abtirsi – naming of paternal lineage

asr – Islamic late afternoon prayer

bajiye – black-eyed pea fritter

bariis – rice

bariis isku karis – one-pot rice and meat

basbaas – hot sauce

burcad badeed – piracy

burjiko – coal stove

cambuulo – adzuki bean dish

canjeero – sour pancake

casariyo – afternoon tea meal

dallac bilaash – tomato sauce

dayr – rainy season

dheri – traditional clay pot

doolsho – cake

fuul – fava bean stew

gashaato/kashaato – coconut dessert

gu – rainy season

hilib – meat

hooyo – mother

iftar – fast-breaking Ramadan meal

jilaal – hot and dry season

kalamuudo – homemade pasta and meat

leeleefow – mango and tamarind chutney

murcood – yellow plum

martiqaad – special gathering with guests

mishaari masaggo – sorghum porridge

muufo – corn flatbread

nafaqo – potato scotch egg

oodkac – beef jerky

qaxwo – coffee

ruwaayad – a play

sambuus – fried dumpling

shaah – spiced Somali tea

sheeko – conversation

Soomaalinimo – Somali identity

soo dhawoow – welcome

soor – corn grits

soor iyo maraq – corn grits and soup

subag – ghee

suqaar – meat and vegetable sauté

suugo – marinara sauce

suuq – market

tinaar – traditional tandoor oven

xawaash – Somalia's seven-spice mix

yicib (yeheb) – Indigenous crop

ACKNOWLEDGMENTS

Ugu horrayn, waxaan u mahadcelinayaa Allah (SWT) oo i siiyay awoodda aan ku qorey buuggan, kaasoo aan si aad ah ugu faraxsanahay in aan qoray. Waxaan buuggan u hibeynayaa gabadhayda qaaliga ah Ruqiyah iyo hooyaday qaaliga ah Xaawo Cabdulle Ducaale oo i bartay wax kasta oo aan garanayo, iina muujisay muhiimadda ay leedahay in la ixtiraamo Soomaalinimada. Iyada taageeradeeda, dhiirigelinteeda, naf hurideeda, dadaalkeeda iyo nolosheyda quruxda badan ma heli laheyn fursadaan quruxda badan, buugaane ma qori laheyn iyada la'aanteed. Mahadsanid hooyo macaan.

Waxaan sidoo kale jeclaan lahaa in aan u mahadceliyo habaryaryaashey ay ugu horeyso Asha Kiin Farah Ducaale, Dahabo Abdulle Ducaale, Khadiijo Abdulle Ducaale, Iska'arag Ali Abdi, Saynab Xabeeb Nur, Farxiyo Fu'aad Hasan, iyo Istahil Cali Cabdi dhamaantood aqoontooda iyo kaalintii ay ka qaateen abuurista buugaan aad iyo aad ayaan ugu mahadnaqayaa. Waayo buugaan suuragal ma ahaan laheyn iyaga la'aantood.

Waxaan buuggan u qoray jacaylka aan u qabo dadkayga Soomaaliyeed. Waxa rajadaydu tahay in buuggeyga cunto karinta ee *Soomaaliya* uu kaalin ka qaato ilaalinta dhaqanka cuntadeena si uu ugu gudbo jiilka xiga, si aan had iyo jeer ugu xirnaano hidaha iyo dhaqanka dheer ee aan ka soo jeedno.

First and foremost I want to thank Allah (SWT) for allowing me to create this book that I am immensely honored to have written. I dedicate this book to my beloved daughter, Ruqiyah—I hope you will use it in the future to remain connected to your dhaqan (culture)—and to my dear mother, Xaawo Cabdulle Ducaale, who taught me everything I know and showed me the importance of always honoring my Somaliniimo. Without your support, encouragement, sacrifice, and dedication to provide me a beautiful life, this book would not exist. Thank you hooyo macaan.

Thank you to my husband, Benjamin Verdoes, for your love, patience, and encouragement throughout this process and for being the first to help me see that my love of writing and passion for the culinary arts were goals worth pursuing. Thank you for also demonstrating in your own work what unrelenting dedication to your craft looks like. With your support and care, I was able to write this book.

Thank you to my best friend, Asiya Gaildon, for encouraging, plotting, and planning alongside me for all of these years. There's no one else I'd rather exchange obscure research emails and long voice memos on ancient Somali history with. We've come so far since our Hart Street days, and I can't wait to read your book.

Thank you to the rest of my family for their support: my baby sister, Hamdi, for her endless championing of me; my dear brothers, Mohamed and Hasan; my sister-in-law, Rukeya; and to my aabo Cabdinaasir. To my cousins Shukri, Sagal, Mulki, I also extend my love.

Thank you to my amazing agent, Clare Mao, for seeing the worth of my work incredibly early on and for helping me bring my dream book to life—I am forever grateful. Thank you to my lovely editor Jenny Wapner for seeing my vision and for believing in the importance and need for this cookbook's existence—it has been a dream come true. Thank you to the incredible Hardie Grant team for all of your hard and valuable work, feedback, and hand in creating this book: in particular my editor Carolyn Insley, Natalie Lundgren, Maddy Kalmowitz, and Louise Newlands. Thank you to my designer Mia Johnson for executing my vision of this book so beautifully.

Thank you to the talented Khadija Farah for adventuring to my hometown of Mogadishu, Somalia, with me and capturing the beauty of our homeland through your stunning images. I am so proud that we shot this book on location in Somalia. I have deep gratitude for all of the kind individuals in Xamar who agreed to be photographed, including many of my cousins and family members.

Thank you to the incredible Doaa Elkady for beautifully photographing the recipes in this book and understanding my vision. I am also immensely grateful to the team that shot the recipes in Brooklyn, New York, for their amazing work and for allowing me to be involved in every step of the process. Thank you to Mallory Lance, Domenique Lanza, Shannon Dowling, and Brett Statman for your incredible food styling work. Thank you to Julia Rose and Kiley Nelson for your prop styling expertise. Thank you to Aziz Farah of Koor Archives for bringing the stunning vintage Somali wares bought back from private European collectors to use in the recipe images—it was an honor to use the beautiful artifacts that our ancestors handcrafted with skill and care. Thank you also to Juba Farms for so kindly supplying the camel meat that we used for the photoshoot.

Thank you to my aunts Asha Kiin Farah Ducaale, Dahabo Abdulle Ducaale, Khadiijo Abdulle Ducaale, Iska'arag Ali Abdi, Saynab Xabeeb Nur, Farxiyo Fu'aad Hasan, and Istahil Cali Cabdi for all of their cultural and culinary knowledge and assistance in creating this book. I am grateful to them, and without them this book would not have been possible.

Thank you to my dear friend Mayukh Sen for your incredible level of support and guidance through the years and for advising me every step of the way, I deeply appreciate you.

I also extend a sincere thank you to Ta-Nehisi Coates, Alicia Kennedy, Fadi Kattan, and Ruby Tandoh for their kind words and support for this book. Thank you for understanding what I set out to accomplish.

Thank you to Dr. Safia Aidid and Dr. Iman Mohamed for your expertise and valuable feedback. Your generosity made it possible to navigate the frustrating lack of accurate written documentations of Somali history. Thank you also to all my online walaalo who answered every email, text, voice note, and call that I had while writing this book. I am grateful for the knowledge and kindness of Ibrahim Hirsi, Huda Hassan, Qaman Omar, Xalane Archives, and Guluf.

Thank you to the inspiring individuals who agreed to be profiled for this book. This book would not be complete without your incredible stories and work: Leyla Adde, Abdullahi Kassim, Barlin Ali, Liban Tahlil, Abdisalan Warsame, Jamal Hashi, Dr. Abdiaziz Hussein Hassan, Ahmed and Abdiasis Ali, Xaawo Mohamed Issa Mohamed, Muhsen Hirabe, Hamda Issa-Salwe, Amal Dirie, and Najiib Abdullahi Mohamud.

Thank you to my wonderful recipe testers whose helpful feedback helped shape the recipes: Mele Girma, Majed Ali, Sara Ahmed, Becky Laird, Maria Amor, Taylor Hunsberger, Valeria Cardenas, Khalid Hussein, Dana Nordenstrom, Burhan Hussein, Jabril "Suldaan" Mohamed Abdullahi.

Thank you to *New York Times Cooking*, where some of the recipes in this book were first published in different iterations. In particular, thank you to my *New York Times* editor Alexa Weibel, who has made me a better recipe developer. I've learned so much from you. Thank you to Emily Weinstein and Genevieve Ko for welcoming me into the *New York Times Cooking* fold as a contributor, which allowed me to strengthen the skills needed to create this book.

Thank you to my generous editors at *TASTE* and *Eater* for allowing me to include my original published essays ("Xawaash Is The Somali Food Blog That Taught a Generation of Diaspora Kids How to Cook" and "On Fusion, Forced Migration, and Somali Food") in this book.

Last but never least, thank you to my dear friends and loved ones: Becky Laird, Gabrielle Rucker, Dylan Rupert, Frances James Dinger, Maria and Jorge Amor, Hanan Diriye, Miski Muse, Judith Killeen, Yewande Komolafe, Jo Marie Riedl, Kaillee Coleman, Jamila Osman, Michelle Schaffner, Kirby Ellis, Tess Herbert, June Canedo de Souza, Bibi Abdulkadir, Nafisa Kaptawalla, Arsh Raziuddin, Saada Ahmed, Ladin Awad, Mohammed Iman Fayaz, Kia Damon, Iman Mohamed, and Marilia Henriquez, Idil Ibrahim, and Gu Isse.

Soomaaliya would not exist without the great efforts and the foundation laid down by pioneers like Asha Mohamud Guled, Barlin Ali, Leyla Adde, and Abdullahi Kassim. I am deeply grateful for their work, their commitment to the preservation of Somali culinary traditions and culture, and for their participation in this book. It is my honor to recognize their legacies in these pages as pioneers of documenting Somali foodways. In particular I thank Barlin Ali and Abdullahi Kassim for helping me understand and see my own work as a continuation of their efforts to ensure Somali culinary traditions make it to the next generation.

I wrote this book out of the love I have for my people, the Somali people. It is my hope that *Soomaaliya* will help us preserve our culinary traditions for the next generation so that we may always remain connected to our shared heritage and the long and proud tradition that we come from. Mahadsanid (thank you) for reading and supporting my work.

INDEX

D

E

T

U

V

W

X

Y

Hardie Grant

NORTH AMERICA

Hardie Grant North America
2912 Telegraph Ave
Berkeley, CA 94705
Hardiegrant.com

Published in the United States by Hardie Grant North America, an imprint of Hardie Grant Publishing Pty Ltd.

MIX
Paper | Supporting responsible forestry
FSC® C020056
FSC
www.fsc.org

Library of Congress Cataloging-in-Publication Data is available upon request.

ISBN: 9781958417836
ISBN: 9781958417843 (eBook)

Printed in China

Design by Mia Johnson

Food styling by Mallory Lance and Domenique Lanza, assisted by Shannon Dowling and Brett Statman

Prop styling by Julia Rose, assisted by Kiley Nelson

First Edition

Ifrah F. Ahmed is a Somali-born, New York-based writer, chef, recipe developer, and artist whose work centers around food, history, culture, memory, and migration. Her writing and recipes have been published in the *New York Times*, where she is a regular contributor, and she has bylines in *Vogue*, *Eater*, *TASTE*, and the *Los Angeles Times*, amongst many others. Her popular Somali culinary pop-up MILK & MYRRH has routinely sold out in Seattle, Los Angeles, and New York, and she has been featured in NPR, *T: The New York Times Style Magazine*, and the *Washington Post*. Named one of *Cherry Bombe's* "Future of Food 50," she is dedicated to the preservation of Somali culinary traditions.